Through The Storm

A Story of Hope, Faith, and Love

Debbie Morgan

Published by Still Standing Publishing Company
Edited by: Bernadine C. Taylor, Literary Services
Back Cover Photo by: Reann Ring (Images by Reann)
Front Cover and Interior Formatting by Still Standing Publishing
Design Team

Printed in the United States of America

ISBN-13: 978-0999336243
ISBN-10: 099933624X

DEDICATION

I dedicate this book to the friends and family that helped me
along the way. Thank you Melayne McInnes, Ellen Marshall
and family & friends for believing in me. When your heart is
broken and you feel discouraged, read Psalm 27 English
Standard Version (ESV)

The LORD is my light and my salvation;
whom shall I fear?
The LORD is the stronghold of my life;
of whom shall I be afraid?
When evildoers assail me
to eat up my flesh,
my adversaries and foes,
it is they who stumble and fall.
Though an army encamp against me,
my heart shall not fear;
though war arise against me,
yet I will be confident.
One thing have I asked of the LORD,
that will I seek after:
that I may dwell in the house of the LORD
all the days of my life,
to gaze upon the beauty of the LORD
and to inquire in his temple.
For he will hide me in his shelter
in the day of trouble;
he will conceal me under the cover of his tent;
he will lift me high upon a rock.

And now my head shall be lifted up
above my enemies all around me,
and I will offer in his tent
sacrifices with shouts of joy;
I will sing and make melody to the LORD.
Hear, O LORD, when I cry aloud;
be gracious to me and answer me!
You have said, "Seek my face."
My heart says to you,
"Your face, LORD, do I seek."
Hide not your face from me.
Turn not your servant away in anger,
O' you who have been my help.
Cast me not off; forsake me not,
O' God of my salvation!
For my father and my mother have forsaken me,
but the LORD will take me in. Teach me your way, O' LORD,
and lead me on a level path
because of my enemies.
Give me not up to the will of my adversaries;
for false witnesses have risen against me,
and they breathe out violence. I believe that I shall look
upon the goodness of the LORD
in the land of the living!
Wait for the LORD;
be strong, and let your heart take courage;
wait for the LORD!

ACKNOWLEDGEMENTS

Thank you to God for helping us through the storms in life. You entrusted us with an amazing story to share and to tell others. We are all so grateful for your protection and guidance.

Thank you to my husband, Steve, for keeping our family together. You have such amazing wisdom and guidance. You are the rock that kept our family together.

Thank you to Ashley for keeping your faith and trusting God through all the trials we faced.

Thank you to my Parents who were always available for whatever we needed. Thank you for your faithful prayers.

Thank you to Pam and John for letting us stay in your home and being such good friends through this process.

Thank you to Riley and Stephanie for the encouragement and love you gave Ashley.

Thank you to Tim for so many special things you did for our family. Thank you mostly for loving and caring for Ashley. Thank you to Lisa for all the walks on this journey and for always checking on me.

Thank you to Mandy for getting the word out there to so many people that helped us.

Thank you to LIFT Ministry and Charlie Conder for all the gift cards.

Thank you to the Dennis family who helped with bedding. We are so grateful for your friendship.

Thank you to Robert for encouraging me to be a witness during this time.

There are so many special friends that we will be forever grateful for your love and kindness.

Thank you to Bob and Connie Morgan for instilling the importance of saving. We are sad that you are not with us but thank you for taking care of us financially through the storms in life.

CONTENTS

CONTENTS

INTRODUCTION

My family consists of Steve, Ashley, and Debbie (me) Morgan. I have been married 28 years to Steve Morgan. Steve is an incredibly smart person that loves building and creating things. He created an R2D2 that is a fully functioning droid, and he drives him around with remote control. He makes sounds that are from the movie Star Wars. He is an exact replica from the movie. Steve made some of his parts using a 3D printer. He printed them in purple filament and then spray painted them either blue or silver. He built the frame using a CNC machine.

Steve built R2 because he had cancer several years ago. When he was diagnosed, we stayed in the hospital for 18 months for his experimental treatments. Times at the hospital were so long, but God healed him of Cancer. Steve takes R2 to brighten the kid's day at hospitals. We take him around to different venues also to help raise money for charities and to make a difference in people's lives.

Steve also built 40 life-sized animals for a company called Sight and Sound. This was for the live production of Noah. At the play, the animals were in the Ark along with real animals. The Ark was all around the audience, and it appeared like we were in the boat. This was amazing to see the hard work he had put in and now to see it in a play. Noah and the animals tell the Biblical story of how Noah builds an Ark.

I have stayed at home with our daughter Ashley Morgan. I taught preschool at Christian schools for many years when she started school. I homeschooled her from 4th to 6th grade and then again from 10th to 12th grade. She graduated from

Abeka Christian Academy in January 2016. After she graduated, I enjoyed helping others. My parents live close by so I often help bring them food and clean their house. I like doing for others.

Ashley is 19, works at a fast food restaurant and helps with worship at our church. She also works with the elementary kids with worship every Sunday. She got a concussion on April 19th, 2016, from dropping a box on her head at work. She has been through physical therapy and vestibular therapy for her eyes. She deals with repercussions of the concussion daily. She constantly has headaches but is earnestly seeking God and feels that she is to worship him even through her pain. She is currently enrolled in Shorter University to study Christian Studies. She is an amazing musician. We have both written several Christian songs together. She is gentle, kind and compassionate. She loves God so much and has been singing in worship since she was little. She started singing in plays at Hebron Church. She has sung at various venues singing Christian music. She started singing harmony when a friend encouraged her to learn it. In high school, she played in the Joyful Noise Homeschool Marching Band. She played clarinet, piccolo, and the flute.

Joyful Noise was about an hour from our house, but we drove there every Friday so she could experience Marching Band. She also was involved in Dancin' Grits which taught High School girls how to dance. At the end of the year, they have a big dance with no dates and have fun with what they have learned. She had some great experiences because she was homeschooled.

She is dating Tim whom she met on a Christian dating site. It was important to her that she date someone that was a Christian. They talked for several months before meeting. She wanted to make sure that he had the same values and upbringing that she did. Tim has been there for Ashley during her concussion and through so many things. We are glad that God sent her someone that would encourage her and love her the way God intended a relationship to be.

We are all involved in an organization called the Georgia 501st. Steve controls R2, Ashley dresses up as Leia, Rey, and a Legacy Storm trooper. I help people in costumes to see and to get dressed. Most of the characters with helmets cannot see; so, I make sure they don't run into anything. For the 501st, we help raise money for different charities like CHOA, Big Bert's Adventure, Make a Wish, Breast Cancer Foundation and lots of other charities.

Our Faith is very important to us all. We attend church each week and we all volunteer. Steve is helping with sound each Sunday. Ashley helps with children and backup vocals, and I sing in the choir. God has brought us through so much and continues to have his protection upon us. The storms in life come and go, but it is our faith that holds us together. Hope you enjoy our true story.

Here is our true story of Through the Storm. Pray God will touch your lives as you read this story and to always keep your Hope, Faith, and Love.

CHAPTER ONE
The Storm

The Lord will watch over your coming and going
both now and forevermore.
Psalm 121:8 (NIV)

Today, August 18th, 2016 at 7:30, we are all sitting down as a family trying to find something to watch on TV. This is an abnormal night because we are all in the living room on the same level. There is a storm outside with thunder and lots of lightning, so we wanted to be together. The lightning strikes are loud and very scary. We took our dog (Leia) downstairs because she is barking so loudly. My family consists of my husband, daughter (19) and myself. We are flipping channels, and there is nothing on. Our show that we want to watch comes on at 8:00 so we start watching a show for a few minutes. The storm stopped there was no lightning, no thunder and no rain. The storm had quietened down and was very still. Little did we know that our lives were about to change forever.

At 7:57, we hear a loud boom right by our outlet in our living room. The outlet right by R2D2 was black, and it looked like it exploded. I screamed who is shooting at R2? The sound was so loud. It sounded like a gunshot. It scared all of us. My husband said to get out of the house that "I think we have a fire. Call 911!" I called but did not report we had a fire. I just needed them to check things out. I did not believe we had a fire because I did not see anything that resembled a fire. We had been hit by lightning before when there was a loud noise, but this noise sounded like a gunshot.

We have been hit two other times, and the lightning just messed up equipment.

I walked outside, but both of us realized we needed to get R2D2 out of the house. R2 is so heavy. I usually cannot lift him without help. Steve and I lifted him down the front stairs and onto the driveway. In the living room near the plug, was the location of the noise. We could visibly see a black mark on the wall. It was imperative to get R2 out. One of our neighbors was outside smoking a cigarette. Steve and I were screaming at our neighbor outside asking for help. He didn't hear us. Then he quickly came over and helped Steve get R2 in the car. Steve and I went down to the basement to get Leia, our dog. We brought her up to the driveway.

We have no electricity, at this point, so my husband gives me a flashlight. He gets the fire extinguisher and heads down to the basement. The fire is in the closet where all the sound equipment is stored. I am holding the flashlight so he can see and he pulls the clip on the fire extinguisher. He is spraying in the area where he thinks there is fire. We still do not visibly see a fire. It is so dark, and it is hard to see anything. Then suddenly the smoke starts getting bad. He tells me to call 911 back again. The operator said the firemen were on their way.

In the meantime, I wanted to go after the items that were important to me. Most things in our house could be replaced or repaired. What is the one thing you would grab? What is so important that you would risk your life for? My pictures were so important to me; so, I went back into the house for pictures that could not be replaced. I go into the house and try to get them in the hall closet downstairs. The smoke becomes so bad, and I can hardly see the pictures. Then I start to find them, but they are too heavy and too many of them. Which one would I choose? How could I just pick one album? The smoke becomes very intense, and I can hardly breathe. I really wanted the pictures and the special memories I have had with my family, but I realize it is too dangerous to be inside the house.

The firemen finally pull up with lots of fire trucks and hoses. They have a total of 4 firetrucks and lots of police. Our road is filled with emergency vehicles. The outside of the house appears to be fine with no visible fire. It was hard to understand at the time why we had so many fire trucks. On the outside of the house, you could not visibly see much. Then suddenly, a big thing of smoke came out the front door. We have smoke because there is a huge fire in our basement. Ashley and I started to become frightened, but we knew that God was with us. We are all scared at this point, and we are not sure what is going to happen.

God is the only one that could help us at this point. Several of our neighbors came down to check on us. We took the dog to our neighbor's house. We moved our cars so fire trucks could get closer to the house. We waited which seemed like forever. At a time like this, all people could do was love on us and pray. My neighbors and I stood out in the cul-de-sac and began to pray. Pray for the workers as they were in a house with a fire. Prayed for our house and prayed for our pictures. The only thing I cared about in the house that day was my pictures. My memories of family time and memories of family members in heaven. Lots of things can be replaced, but pictures to me were something that could never be replaced. While the fire is going on, I begin to text people and ask them to pray. My Mom always taught me when faced with adversity and hard situations to get a prayer chain going. I called my Mom first and asked her to pray. I texted more neighbors, and they came to our house and loved on us. All I could think to do while waiting was pray and to trust God. Yes, we were all very frightened, but we knew that when we seek God and get a prayer chain going, that he would answer our prayers.

The smell of the smoke was so bad we decided to wait in the cars. At this point, we all must keep our faith, that no matter the outcome that God is with us. We were surrounded by people that loved us. Our friends waited with us the whole time and never left our side. One of the most touching calls was from our Pastor. He said the church would help us with anything we needed. My Mother also called and wanted to come to us, but she could not physically get through on the street. My Mom also has oxygen and thought it would be dangerous for her to be around all the smoke. For a long time, Ashley was in the car by herself. She was so scared of what was going to happen to our house. I reminded her that we have each other and that was the most important thing; we are all blessed to be alive. Ashley has asthma, and the smoke was making her cough and have a hard time breathing. Tim, her boyfriend, was texting her and helping her to stay calm. She also talked to her Grandma to help comfort her.

There was no way to get down the street because of all the fire trucks and police cars. The only people that could come to the scene were our immediate neighbors.
It took several hours to put the fire out. The firemen took 10 minutes to get there, but the fire was so involved by that time. The fire was in the basement in the closet, the firemen

said. The firemen were spraying water in the basement, and there were also firemen in the living room upstairs. The firemen told us at this point that "you cannot go back into the house," that is was not safe. They did advise us that we needed to get valuables and any jewelry on the second floor only. This was the only area that was safe. Everything looked the same on the second floor, but the smoke smell was bad. It was so hard to breathe when we walked in. You could see soot when you moved items. We were all so grateful to be alive. We were all in a state of shock. How do you think about the valuables in your home? We grabbed expensive jewelry and some other items. It is so hard to mentally process grabbing valuables, but we do the best we can.

Our Adjuster from our insurance company personally called to make sure we were being taken care of. He assured me that the insurance company would walk us through the process and would take care of us every step of the way. He wanted us to stay in a hotel that night, but we didn't have any essential items. We have clothes that smell like smoke, no toothbrush, hair brush and nothing to sleep in. At this point, it is about 10:00 at night, and we are all shock about what has happened. Without hesitation, my friend Pam offered for us to stay at her house. We were all so overwhelmed that Pam and John would let us stay with them. They brought us to their home and gave us clothes and essential items for the night. They have a beautiful home, and Ashley had a beautiful guest room with a bathroom. We had a huge bonus bedroom. We had a very nice bed, TV, and a bathroom. We were so grateful for their kindness and support.

They told us that we could stay until we figured things out with the house. Stephanie is their daughter, and she lives in the basement along with Riley, her friend. When they came home that night, I said, "Well you all wanted us all to get together so here we are." In every situation, Steve and I tried to find something positive. There is always something to be thankful for. Stephanie and Riley were so surprised that we were not more shaken up about the fire. Having the fire was emotional but being surrounded by friends made everything so much easier. Each day we would all get together, talk and laugh. It was so comforting to be around people who love and care for us; something a hotel could have never done. We are so thankful to the Fosters for their love and friendship.

Because the fire happened on a Thursday, this gave us time over the weekend to process. To get prayed up for what we were about to face. That night we begin to cry because of all we had been through. We knew God would take care of us. We began to let people know and ask for prayers. Steve and I knew we had to pray about how to handle the trials we were to face. We always try to handle everything with a positive, uplifting attitude. It is sometimes hard to find the positive in some situations. One positive, I know, is that God saved us from the storm that day. We are all very grateful to be alive. We know the seriousness of the fire we had in our home. We are all extremely blessed to have each other, and everything else can be replaced.

On Monday morning, the insurance company sends out an adjuster to our house to assess the damage. It was hard walking back into our home and seeing the damage. We have a two-story house with a basement. First, we walk into the main level. The dining room and my office look the same, but the smoke smell is so strong! It is hard to walk through the house because of the smell. I walked into the living room, and there is a big hole in the living room floor. I start getting closer because I wanted to see. The adjuster warned me that the floor was unstable and he did not want me to get too close. In the hole, you could see parts of the basement, and it was a little concerning because the floor was not strong. Lots of items had been broken because the firefighters were on the main level and basement trying to put out the fire.

Upstairs in our room, everything looked the same except if you moved something you could see the soot from the smoke. All the cabinets, floors and pretty much everything was covered in soot. I knew the basement was going to look very scary, so I saved looking at it for last. Only God could have prepared me for what I saw. Everything looked so black and so burned. Our ceiling was all over the room. The fire started in the gas line, which was in the ceiling. So, we had insulation on the ground and all our black ceiling tiles from the media room. The brown couches were ruined because of everything that fell on them. Our oriental rug had pieces of the ceiling and insulation on it as well. To make sure the firemen had the fire out they had to punch holes into the drywall. There was so much damage to the basement. Steve's workshop area appeared to be fine. He had an enormous amount of soot damage, but he was hoping everything would still work. Steve's recording equipment was on a table downstairs. The fire was right above this table, so the equipment had a lot of water damage.

The adjusters started talking to us about the claim on the house. We will have two adjusters one for the structure of the house and one for the contents of our home. They assured us that we had enough coverage for the contents and the structure of our home. It was very educational to find out that we had more money to work with if the house is repaired vs. rebuilt. However, the house had so much damage. Our adjusters were not sure if they were going to fix the existing house. The floor damage is hard to repair since we have 12 ft. ceilings in the house. That is why the floors were so dangerous. If you fell in the hole, you would fall 12 ft. into the basement. Steve and I begin to pray about the process. To repair or to rebuild would both take about six months. God knew the outcome and knew what we would face. Now we had to trust him with this process and know without a doubt he would take care of us. In Philippians 4:6-7 NIV, "Do not be anxious about anything, but in every situation, by prayer and petition, with thanksgiving, present your requests to God. And the peace which passeth all understanding shall keep your hearts and minds through Jesus Christ."

So, there are several companies that came each day. We have a company who packs up all the contents of your home. We did not get a chance to go through anything. So, they packed up our house exactly as we left it. All the junk drawers were all packed. All the stuff we were holding on to that did not matter to us. All of our contents were going to get packed and get cleaned. This company packed all the hard items in the house. Another company would get the soft stuff like clothing, towels, linens, and curtains. They also asked us to get out emergency clothing. Ashley needed to have her uniform for work the next day. We also needed clothes that we could wear each day. I had an extremely hard time thinking of what we would need for six months. I grabbed a few outfits. Steve has just made a Jedi costume for the 501st. He was so excited that he had finished most of it. We also sent this and Ashley's Rey costume to get cleaned. As I am looking through items to take, I realize we had so many clothes and items we didn't wear. So, I started going through items, and I made a huge pile of clothes and items that I did not want. The electronics were picked up by ERS, and they would test each piece to see if it will work.

Building relationships were important to me so; I talked to each person that came in the house. I tried to find out their story and what I could pray for in their lives. People said we should pray for you. I told them I would appreciate the prayers, but I wanted to know what I could pray for them. I told them our house could be repaired or replaced. All the items in this house are just stuff. It is not what is important in life; and that our family is most important and our relationship with God. I learned each one of their names and tried to call them by name. There were four girls with contents company, and I really enjoyed getting to know each one of them. We took selfies together and had so much fun talking. We laughed and had a great time together. They packed up our stuff, but I talked to them while they were working. They made comments about how I was so positive. I told them that God saved our family from the fire. I told them how blessed we all were to be alive. I talked to them about God and each one of their lives. The struggles they faced. I earnestly began praying and seeking God for each person.

One of the most impactful conversations was with the adjuster for the structure of our home. He said people would be watching you through this and how you conduct yourself. You will impact more people during the process of this fire than you will your entire life. You can be a witness to others and tell people what God has done for you. I started praying that I would be a witness to others through the fire and they would see the light of Jesus in my life. Each day we all have an opportunity to be an impact unto the world. We all have good news to share. Keeping our focus on God and not our trials is important. Don't let trials consume you. Find the good in the situation. Sometimes it may be hard but know that God is with you each step of the way. I began to get excited that God entrusted me with such an amazingly powerful story. I get to share this story for life!

Investigation day was a reality to us of how blessed we all are to be alive. The inspector told us that the lightning hit a gas line. The lightning hit the flex pipe that goes to the fireplace. Because it hit the area, it poked holes in the pipe, and it ignited gas at the same time. Thus, turning it into a flamethrower underneath the wood floors. We had paint cans, gasoline, acetone in close proximity to the fire. The inspector said, 'how did this house not blow up?' There are so many things down here that should have ignited the fire and caused the house to blow up. He was very surprised that we had anything left to the house. This put into reality of how God protected us and kept us safe. God gave us a truly amazing story to share with others. He protected us when in the world's view said we should not have made it. I told the examiner that day that God protected us, and He was the only reason we were still here. The inspector was here to make sure that we had not started the fire but also, he was here to investigate the gas pipe. The inspector said that the gas line was a faulty gas pipe. Basically, the gas line was manufactured too thin. The lightning came down the chimney and went down to the gas line, and it sparked over to the ground and that put holes in the gas line. So, the gas line had little tiny holes in it, and that was releasing gas into the air. Steve and I were down in the basement when gas was in the air. Our lives were at risk at the time of the fire. We are all so grateful to God for his protection. It really put things into perspective the seriousness of the fire.

He began to tell us that the house was an investigation site and that no one could tamper with anything in the basement. We were not allowed in the basement area for any reason until the investigation was over. The gas line is now under investigation, and they could possibly sue the manufacturer. So, the next few days, people are coming out to look at the pipe and to determine whether they have a case for suing the manufacturer.

God has an amazing plan for our lives. He saved us through this storm and gave us shelter in our time of need. He knew the trials we would face and the burdens we would bare. He gave us strength and courage as only He could give. We were only strong because of God helping us through each step of the way. We know that our God will supply all our needs. He is faithful to us, and we shall remain faithful to Him. Every situation that arises we know that we must keep the Faith and share our story.

Journal Entry:
Psalm 77 reminds me that my comfort comes from God. I am reminded to remember the works of the Lord and what he has done for us. Verse 12 KJV "I will meditate of thy good work and talk of thy doings." My help comes from the Lord.

David writes Psalm 27 not during a storm but when he came out of it. God can work through our trials. David kept having repetitive trials, and so have we. We need to trust God and keep our faith in him. Psalm has been our encouragement through the storms in life.

Phil4:6-7 NIV "Do not be anxious about anything by prayer and petition, with thanksgiving, present your requests to God. And the peace of God, which transcends all understanding, will guard your hearts and your minds in Christ Jesus."

CHAPTER TWO
The Process Begins

The steps of a good man are ordered by the Lord:
and he delighteth in his way.
Psalm 37:23 (KJV)

We have been staying with our friends since the fire. Dealing with the fire issues we needed to be at our house daily. It was very convenient to stay in the neighborhood during the beginning stages. My neighbor Mandy set up a site on FB for people to help us. We had people that we did not know giving us gift cards for restaurants. At the beginning stages, friends came by to bring dinners to the Foster's house for everyone. People were so kind and helpful. We had the Geekspace come over and help us with some of Steve's equipment to try to clean it up and save it. They worked so hard trying to help Steve. They let him store equipment at Geekspace to see if items were repairable, but most of the equipment rusted from the water damage. So many people are asking what they can do to help. It is so touching to see that so many people care. We are so grateful that people are going out their way to help us.

Ashley's (our daughter) first day of college was the day of the fire. Stephanie and Riley were trying to help her. Mandy, our neighbor, gave her school supplies. She tried for about a week. She was too overwhelmed for her to be successful at school. So, she dropped out of college. At first, she was very sad but realized it was the best decision. The first time she signed up for college she got a concussion and now the fire on her second attempt. She feels like God doesn't want her to go to college right now.

Stephanie is the Foster's daughter and Riley lives with them. Both have been really good friends to Ashley for quite some time. Her boyfriend, Tim, has been so encouraging and concerned for her as well. He has been there, right by her side, through her concussion and now the fire. God has placed an amazing man in her life at a perfect time. He has been there to encourage her and to be a great friend to her. We thank God for the friends that have been there for her every step of this trial. She has had a hard time understanding why this has happened. God has placed the right people to lift her up during this trying time.

It took the contents company several weeks to pack up the house. The soft clothes item company came out each day too. We had an enormous amount of clothes, sheets, rugs, etc. in the house. The Electronic company came to pick up all the electronics in a van. They apparently did not warn him that we had an enormous amount of electronics. He had to come back with a much bigger truck. My husband had sound equipment for running live shows, TV's, mics and lots of equipment.

Each Restoration company took them several weeks to get everything out of the house. Each day Steve and I would come by the house to check on the progress. I loved talking to each person that came in the house. Steve and I were positive through the process. I loved taking selfies with the girls that took the contents of our home. I also talked to the guy taking our clothes apologizing for all he had to pack up. I am a helper so watching everyone pack the house is quite difficult for me. So, I started going through some of the clothes and begin to clean out rooms. I gave a lot of formal dresses and anything I did not wear to Quinn House a local homeless charity. The soft clothes guy told me he didn't mind taking whatever I needed to be cleaned, but I thought it was wasteful for him to pack up clothes I would never wear.

The girls from the contents company worked so extremely hard each day. They were covered in soot and didn't mind the enormous amount of stuff they had to pack up. However, it was so funny when they said, "Mrs. Morgan how many sets of dishes do you have?" I have one set of everyday dishes, Easter dishes, Christmas dishes and two sets of China. All of them had a place setting for 8. It was a lot of dishes. They would often tease me of why I needed so many dishes. We all had so much fun together. Each day I took it as an opportunity to learn a little about each one of them. I prayed for their protection and prayed for their individual needs. I prayed that each one of them could see Christ in me and that I was being a good witness to them.

During this time, God impressed upon me to think of others better than myself. To think of peoples' stories and what they are going through. A house can be rebuilt, but there are some people in the world that are hurting and that don't know Him. He brought the passage Philippians 2:3-4 NIV to heart, "Do nothing out of selfish ambition or vain conceit. Rather, in humility value others above yourselves, for not looking to your own interests but each of you to the interests of the others." It helped me realize to think of others better than myself and to take each person I meet as an opportunity to spread God's love.

As I come back to the house and begin sorting through our stuff, I realize that stuff does not matter. Why were we saving all this stuff? I have baby clothes and baby toys from my daughter. She is 19 years old, and I have saved it all these years. Why? Did I really think she would use them for her kids? We all have so much stuff that we never used and often I felt like it was consuming us. You see before the fire, I wanted to start getting rid of stuff and cleaning out, but we all wanted to hang on to those precious memories and stuff. My In-laws passed away in 2009 from cancer, and all of us wanted to hang on to the things they had because it reminded us of them. We had coats that had their smell.

Special items that could never be replaced from them. Once items are cleaned, they will no longer have "their" smell. Most of these items have smoke damage from the fire, but we will always have them in our hearts. God has blessed us with a beautiful home and a lot of stuff. It is time for us as a family to bless others with the stuff we don't use. There are so many hurting people out there that don't have the essential items. We are all thankful that we can bless others with essential items they may need.

During this time, we have been away from our home, we have had the bare minimum of things we needed. So, at Church, I have a small girls group, and we started making Ziploc bags full of essential items a person would need if they were homeless. The small group girls and I have made scarves before, but now I knew what it felt like to be homeless. We all took for granite the everyday things we use, and now we had an opportunity to help others. We put toothpaste, toothbrushes, food item, soap and shampoo in each bag. Each person would hand out a bag when they saw someone on the street when driving around town. We all see the homeless person on the side of the street but how often do we help? This was a way we could give and to help the ones in need. We have come to realize how much we can do without and what matters in life. We were all saved that day from the fire. We were all alive and well and that is something to be truly grateful for. We all have our relationship with God which can never be taken away.

The Contents company are going through items in the house and packing up most of it, and then they go to the basement. The basement was the most damaged area. You can see the soot from the fire and the damage to the house. There are contents of the house all in our media room. Most of Steve's equipment was ruined in the fire. His CNC machine and his 3D printers are all ruined because of the fire. Both of us were having a hard time processing all that had been lost. It was quite overwhelming. So, we are all going through contents that were in the basement. Steve had about 300 boxes in the basement alone. One of the girls asked me, "What do you want me to do with this pirate ship?" I can't clean that. Out of all the things in our house that had been damaged, this is the one item that made me cry. Steve had put this pirate ship together when he was in the hospital taking chemo. It was a reminder of what God had brought us through. How we had such tremendous faith through the trial of cancer and how he was healed through our faithful Father. She saw that this was a struggle for us and she took the pirate ship to see what she could do.

Most of the items that the electronic company tested did not work so we chose to get a storage unit so that Steve could go through each individual equipment. We had to also find a place for everything in the garage. None of the companies cleaned out the garage. We also had to clean out the refrigerator as well. All the food in the house had to be gone through. Nothing in plastic containers could be saved. Any items in paper or boxes would have to be gotten rid of. All the appliances were ruined and not able to be saved. We had an electronic company deliver the equipment to the storage unit to help save money for the insurance company. Saving money and not wasting money was very important to both of us. We knew it was the insurance money, but we did not want to be wasteful. In the storage unit, we stored all the electronics and our wave runner.

We had an attic in our basement above Steve's office. Steve worked from home, so he had phone systems and lots of expensive equipment with work. Most of the equipment seems to be ruined. The contents company started pulling items from the attic down. This was another sad moment for us. The plastic containers were all melted. You could barely see the contents that were in each container. ALL our Christmas items were not savable. Ashley's keepsakes and memories that we had saved, all had fire damage. I had saved the dress she came home from the hospital in and special memories. One thing I ask them to try to clean was dolls that her Grandmother had made. See, stuff didn't matter to us, but these special memories did matter. These things were somehow a way of keeping those special memories alive. In James 1:2 NIV, it says to, "Count it all joy when you face trials of many kinds." So, I took pictures each of the special items.

We choose to be joyful and to be positive through this storm. Joyful of all the special relationships and Joyful that we could take a pictures and still remember. Pictures will help keep those memories alive.

We have been staying with the Fosters for a couple of weeks now. It has been great staying there, but they are getting ready to go out of town for Labor Day Weekend. We are scheduled to be in a parade that will be on TV for our first time. We are all excited to be in the Children's Healthcare Parade. Ashley dressed up as Rey and Steve took R2. Instead of staying with the Fosters, we decided to get a hotel and be closer to the interstate. We stayed near the Gwinnett Arena for a few days and then moved to another hotel closer to home. The Fosters went out of town for their Anniversary and Steve did not feel comfortable being there while they were out of town.

Steve is still trying to work during the fire. His job gave us some money to help with expenses. Also, I put out on FB that we had a fire, so our church and neighbors gave us gift cards for food and expenses. We are so extremely grateful for the outpouring of love. We can't rent a house because we could not find anyone that would rent for six months. All the apartments I have been to will not work for us. Both of us do not want to impose on our friends much longer. They are going out of town for a couple of weeks soon, and Steve and I wanted to be settled before they left. Pam and I went looking one day and found the perfect apartment, but it was not available. I began praying about it and seeking God. I asked Steve to meet me over there one day. He did not have a lot of time because he was on his lunch break. I was dealing with questions regarding the house, so I left late. As I was riding, I called the housing guy trying to see our budget. As I began to call, I hit another car. I took the curve too sharp and tapped the car next to me. I begin to ask God why? I felt like we had enough that we had to deal with. My husband was waiting on me, and now I was going to be extremely late. The lady that I hit was having her own struggles. She was trying to get to her Mother that had just had an accident. She was very angry with me that I was not paying attention. She called the police, and an Officer came on a motorcycle. I began to tell the Officer what we had been through and apologized for the inconvenience. Then I asked him if he went to the Chick-fil-a in Lawrenceville. Lots of the Cops from Lawrenceville go there every morning. This store gives them free food, and I told him that my daughter worked there. I described her as the skinny blond girl. He said, "You mean Taylor?" No, her name is Ashley. "Are you talking about the girl that looks like Taylor Swift that works right by the hospital? No, her name is Taylor." All the cops call her Taylor. I did not realize my daughter was known by Taylor and not Ashley. See a lot of people think she looks like Taylor Swift. The Cop said I could write you a ticket for so many things, but I think you are going through enough. Tell Taylor I said, "Hello." I am thanking God the whole way. Thankful for His protection because it could have been so much worse. Thankful I did not get a ticket. I began praying for the ladies' Mother and also began praying about this apartment situation.

So, I start driving to the apartment, which is about 20 minutes away. I called my husband before I left and he says there are no apartments here and it is a waste of time. I wanted to come anyway to see options. We talk to the agent on duty. He said I just don't have anything available and I am not sure about whether the internet would be fast enough for you. Just as we are about to leave a resident from Charter Communications comes out and explains the internet to my husband. Steve says I think that will work, but they don't have any apartments in the time frame we needed. It would be two more weeks before we could move in at this apartment. I know our friends won't mind, but they have been so gracious, and we don't want to impose. Also, Steve had to get back to work, and it was hard without equipment and space. The agent went away to check one more time. I have been praying for weeks for God to lead us to the apartment that would be best for our family. The agent then said, "I can't believe this, but we have one apartment available on the 5th floor." Do you have an elevator? "Yes, we do!" Thank God, we had found a place where we could live, and we could move in within a couple of days. If I would not have been in the accident, then we wouldn't have seen the Charter guy to ask questions. Also, the apartment just became available that day at that timing. God is so Good!! Gods timing is so perfect!! Sometimes we must wait on his timing! I wouldn't have appreciated the apartment as much as I did if we had not gone through this process. He answered all my requests!!

It is a three bedroom, with High spend internet, an elevator (which is not easy to find anywhere), somewhat close to our house and it is so close to Tim. Thank God, for your perfect plan! It has the most beautiful entrance. Full of pretty flowers on both sides. The name of the apartments is The Overlook. It reminds me of how we can overlook the beauty and the blessings. After we moved in, I tried to remind myself of how blessed we are to be at the apartment. The kitchen is right as you walk in. It is a nice size kitchen, too, full of appliances. The washer and dryer are off the kitchen which is perfect for our dog Leia. There is also linoleum on the floors, in the kitchen, so we will use a gate to keep her in that area. She still is not potty-trained. We have a nice big living room with a deck off the back. When we walk from the kitchen, there are two rooms to the left that share a bathroom. Ashley will have the smaller room and Steve will have the bigger room so that he can set up his office and work. The bigger room had a vent in the room, and it was noisy, so it was perfect for Steve. The master bedroom is to the right. We have a gym and a nice swimming pool on the property. It is a very nice apartment, and we are so fortunate to have something so nice during this transition. The location is perfect!! It is close to our Church and to Tim. Thanking God for his perfect plan!

Now the moving process would begin. Wait! Moving? This is going to be the easiest move ever! We bought a few clothes with our gift cards, but we don't have a lot of stuff. We could carry all our belongings in a Large Utility Tote which we did not fill up. All of our stuff got moved in; in one trip. Now Steve would have to figure out how to work from an apartment. He needs to buy new equipment and get new phones. He begins the process and is up and running in a few days.

So now we have a housing person that will help us get items to rent for the apartment. The Housing guy provided us with everything we would need for the next few months. Dishes, towels, sheets, couch, and beds. We slept on beds for a few nights, and it was like sleeping on a board. Everything is rental. I called our friend Bridgette at Sleep Center in Athens, Georgia. I asked them if we could purchase the mattresses that we had bought before. They looked up the invoice, and we had a mattress the next day. Love Brigette, Lee, Devin, and Sierra, we are all so grateful for their friendship. Extremely grateful they could deliver a mattress, so we could all sleep. We had to pay for it ourselves but will be reimbursed when the house is done. Everything the rental company brought for us was white. White Sheets, White bedspread, White towels, White Kitchen towels. We felt like we were in a hotel again and not home. We ended up staying in a hotel about a week since we couldn't find an apartment before our friends left. Thankfully, we were given gift cards from Church so that we could get some cheap comforters from Target and some pillows on clearance. Also, the rental company provided most things, but we did have to buy a lot of essentials. (Soap, shampoo, toothpaste, toilet brush, plunger, etc.) See everything that was in plastic bottles at our house could not be saved. Apparently, the smoke damages items in plastic but not if it was in the glass. Most of our essential items were in plastic and not safe to use. We are all so grateful to the LIFT Ministry at Grayson United Methodist Church, friends, neighbors and total strangers for all the gift cards. This helped us to buy the basic essential items which was very helpful.

I felt like we would all feel better if we just added some color. My Mom loves color and Steve's Mom also used to say color is cheerful. So, I began adding color, and suddenly our temporary home started feeling much better. We got teal comforter with teal and white pillows for our room. We got a coral comforter with coral and white pillows for Ashley. All on clearance. We were also able to get a shower curtain that had scripture on it. To remind us to believe, encourage us to serve others, to praise him and most importantly to trust. Ashley got a shower curtain with lots of corals, teal, green and some yellow. We added some color very cheaply. Made it feel a little more like home. This color would also be used as a blanket during the winter months. The Rental company provided us with a comforter for the bed but did not give us any blankets. My Mom ended up buying us each a blanket and with color!

One thing we all realized is that stuff does not matter in life; it is what is in our hearts that matter. Having a relationship with God and knowing that he will always take care of us is the most important thing in life. As well as relying on God and praying through adversity. I leaned on Him when I couldn't find an apartment, and He provided a place for us to live. His timing was perfect, and I realized that, because of the accident. I appreciated the apartment more because I knew that it came from God. It is imperative that we seek God's desires for our lives. God has so many wonderful things for all of us. Psalm 121 NIV, tells us to "Lift our eyes unto the Lord because that is where our help comes from." So, it is important for me to keep my eyes on him and not on material things that will waste away.

We lost a lot of material things the day of the fire, but we still have each other. We choose to be positive and to seek God through this trial. We have chosen the way of truth, and we are running with endurance "the race that is set before us, Looking to Jesus the author and the finisher of our faith." Hebrews 12:1-2 NIV. The only thing that matters in life is our relationship with God and others. Our relationship with God is personal, and it can never be taken away.

Journal Entry:

I am reminded today that material things do not matter. Our family escaped the fire and we were all safe. Things can be replaced but people cannot. Also, I am reminded that our relationship with God is one thing that people cannot take away from us. There is no safety in things. 1st Timothy 6:9.

God is teaching me things I could have only learned through the fire. I have witnessed and encouraged so many with our story of hope. I remember today that when God closes one chapter of your life that he opens a new chapter. There are usually new experiences, new hope, and a fresh start. Usually, there is something better ahead of you. When God closes one door, he opens another for you. I am finding HOPE in God and His promises. Life changes all the time, whether it's a fire, health, divorce, etc. We must keep hope and faith in him through EVERY circumstance.
Matthew: 6:19-21 Lay not up for yourselves treasures upon earth, where moth and rust doth corrupt, and where thieves break through and steal:

Matthew 6:33 But seek ye first the kingdom of God, and his righteousness; and all these things shall be added unto you.

Matthew 16:26 For what is a man profited, if he shall gain the whole world, and lose his own soul? Or what shall a man give in exchange for his soul?

Isaiah 22:22 When he opens doors, no one will be able to close them; when he closes doors, no one will be able to open them.

Psalm 136:1 NIV Give thanks unto the Lord for he is good. His love endures forever.

Isaiah 48:17 NIV I am the Lord your God who teaches you what is best for you, who directs you in the way you should go.

Matthew 7:7-8 (NIV) Ask and it will be given to you; seek and you will find; knock and the door will be opened to you. [8] For everyone who asks receives; the one who seeks finds; and to the one who knocks, the door will be opened.

Psalm 121:1-3 (KJV) I will lift up mine eyes unto the hills, from whence cometh my help. My help cometh from the LORD, which made heaven and earth. He will not suffer thy foot to be moved: he that keepeth thee will not slumber.

CHAPTER THREE
Rebuild or Repair

For God alone, O my soul, wait in silence,
for my hope is from him.
He only is my rock and my salvation,
my fortress; I shall not be shaken.
On God rests my salvation and my glory;
my mighty rock, my refuge is God.
Trust in him at all times, O' people;
pour out your heart before him;
God is a refuge for us. Selah
Psalm 62:5-8 (ESV)

After the contents of the house are taken out, we must decide on a company that will start the rebuilding process. Our Insurance company wants to rebuild instead of tearing the whole house down and start over. Our Insurance company sends the contents company out to see if they would be interested in repairing the home since they also have people who repair houses. It is a dangerous job because there is a big hole in the living room floor. The contents company said they felt uncomfortable taking the job. We met with several other contractors; that the Insurance company recommended but most of the companies did not want to attempt to repair our home. The Insurance adjuster told us this would take a specialized contractor and that not anyone would attempt to repair the floor. We have several friends that are great contractors, and we know they would do a great job, but were concerned about the repairing of the floor. The Insurance Advisor advised us not to use a smaller company because we needed someone skilled in replacing the floor and some of the framing. The Contractor that our insurance recommended felt very confident about repairing the floor and they had all the contractors we would need. They would handle the process of cleaning up the home and repairing. Steve was not able to meet with the contractor that day because he was working. I hired the contractor to begin the repairing process. The contractor is a good Christian man, and I felt confident that he would take care of us. They said it would take about six months to repair the house. So, that meant that we would be in the apartment six months.

The Insurance company talked to us about the claim being a small loss claim at the beginning. As the investigation is taking process, the adjusters begin to realize all of what was involved in repairing our home. It is going to take $156,000 to repair the structure of our home. We have a $42,000 of depreciation to our home. They did not realize a number of expensive possessions we had in our home which would also cost to replace. On a fire claim you have a certain amount for structure and then another amount for contents. The Contents Agent switched it to a large claim because of all the extensive damage to our home. Thankfully we had enough insurance to cover the structure of our home and the contents of our home. Each item in our home will have a depreciation value depending on how long we have had the items. We know that God is in this process and will take care of us along the way.

We did not realize how long it would take for the process to begin on our home. The contractor I hired was the Manager, and so he does not come out to the site for the process. He has a Contract Manager that will oversee the project. The Project Manager will find the workers for flooring, painting, and reconstruction of our home.

The investigation took a while. We had the house fire on August 19, and the process did not start until October 20th. During this time, the workers are cleaning up the mess in the basement and carrying it to the dumpster. They filled up several dumpsters with all the discarded items just from the basement, alone. It was so hard to put special memory items in the dumpster. Each day, I would have to come over and start going through documenting the items that we were discarding. These two months also gave us time to get Steve back to work and 'up and running.' We moved into the apartment on September 12th, and we were all excited about our temporary home. It was right next to the Gwinnett Braves. It is a very nice area of town and convenient to everything. Ashley is excited because it is closer to Tim and it would be more convenient for him. When we were looking for the apartments that was one of the criteria that it was close to Tim.

On October 20th, 2016, the demolition process begins. The walls in the living room, half bath and office are coming down. The dining room and kitchen area walls will stay up. All the bedroom walls are all fine, but they will need to be painted with special paint. In the basement, all the walls must come down. All the carpet, hardwoods, and tile must be pulled up in the entire house. The first day, there are people everywhere, in the house. People are pulling up floors and nails. People knocking out walls. Most of the people don't speak English, so it is hard to talk to anyone. All the walls get knocked down, and you can walk through the whole house.

When I look outside of our house, it looks as if everything is fine. On the inside of our house, it is a mess. We have drywall everywhere, ripped up flooring, and the basement still has ceiling tiles and debris from the fire removed. They have taken up our couches and things that were destroyed, but it still looks and smells very bad. This is kind of like our lives as Christians. Some of us are an emotional wreck, a mess on the inside, but on the outside, we are all put together. We go to church, and we put on a happy smile, but on the inside, we are a mess and hurting. We are all hurting in different ways. It is hard to expose yourself to others and to express your concerns. To break the walls down and be real with each other. People do not always take time to get to know each other. People are busy on their phones in this generation and don't realize that relationships are what matters in life. Taking time to love people. All of us just want to feel loved and cared for. If we take time to get to know each other, we might realize that we have the same struggles.

We know that we are not the only one going through a difficult time. God impressed upon me the importance of thinking of others better than myself. Through this process, I have begun trying to get to know people and to encourage them through THEIR storm. To love them for who they are and try to lift them up through their difficulties.
Outward appearances do not tell someone if you are a follower of Christ. But how you treat others and react to situations shows people that there is something different in you. The peaceful look on your face and the outpouring of love demonstrates your love of Christ. I have tried to be peaceful and positive through the adversity. I am so grateful

that the Structure Adjustor reminded me at the beginning of the fire that my attitude would matter to others. The life you lead reflects a life for Christ or the enemy. One or the other. Which do you choose when life gets messy like our house? God has transformed my life through this fire. I have been more of a witness for Him through this fire and through this storm. I am grateful for this storm in life and can't wait to see what God is going to do.

It is good to keep our eyes focused on God. He is the only one that can help us with the mess. We all need to let our walls down and be vulnerable to each other and let people in our lives. You never know when you share your story how much it can encourage and lift someone up. Imagine if David would not have shared his story of his different emotions. We would have a piece of the Bible missing. Sharing your story shows people that God is real and he will take care of you through the trials in life.

The inside of our house is where we spend time with others and build relationships. It is where people feel comfortable and can let their guard down and be real with us. We have people and friends over all the time at our home. We have so much laughter and fun. We know with this mess we have in our home, that it will be hard to continue building those friendships. We must find joy in the mess and our circumstances. Our true friends will be around; our house will get repaired, and one day soon, we will be home. It is so important to find the positive in every situation. God protected us that day from the fire, and I am so grateful for the life lessons he has taught me 'through the fire and through this storm.'

Journal Entry:

God, you have taught me so many things. One is to cherish the life you have given us because it could be taken away in the blink of an eye. Thank you for saving us on 8/18/16 from the fire. You have blessed our family so much with life and now a place to live. You taught me, Lord, that the outside of our house looked perfect. It was unharmed. No visible damages but the inside was full of ashes and destruction. You taught me that everyone is hurting on the inside of our hearts but all in different ways. Our living room floor had a hole in the middle of the floor. It reminded me as a Christian the hole that we try to fill with so many things. You are the only person that can truly fill in that hole in our lives and help us with the mess in our lives. Praying for people as they read this book to fully rely on you through the storms in life. Praying that as they go through difficulties, they know that you are with them.

God is faithful when the future is uncertain. God is faithful when I am unfaithful. I praise you today for your faithfulness and protection. Thank you for your love and comfort. Thank you for your forgiving heart.

Journal Entry:
Scriptures were what helped me through the storms in life. Seeking God daily in his word and praying. Sometimes I did not know how to pray so I prayed the word.

Psalm 57:1-3 (NIV) Have mercy on me, my God, have mercy on me, for in you I take refuge.
I will take refuge in the shadow of your wing until the disaster has passed. I cry out to God Most High, to God, who vindicates me. He sends from heaven and saves me, rebuking those who hotly pursue me—God sends forth his love and his faithfulness.

Message Version: Verse 9-10 - I'm thanking you, God out loud on the streets singing your praises in town and country. The deeper your love, the higher it goes; every cloud is a flag to your faithfulness.

God will supply all your needs according to his riches and glory in Christ Jesus. Phil 4:19 KJV

CHAPTER FOUR
Foundation

"When he was in the cave. A prayer.
I cry aloud to the LORD;
I lift up my voice to the LORD for mercy.
I pour out before him my complaint;
before him I tell my trouble.
When my spirit grows faint within me,
it is you who watch over my way.
In the path where I walk
people have hidden a snare for me.
Look and see, there is no one at my right hand;
no one is concerned for me.
I have no refuge;
no one cares for my life.
I cry to you, LORD;
I say, "You are my refuge,
my portion in the land of the living.
Listen to my cry,
for I am in desperate need;
rescue me from those who pursue me,
for they are too strong for me.
Set me free from my prison,
that I may praise your name.
Then the righteous will gather about me
because of your goodness to me."
Psalm 142 (NIV)

The first step is to get the foundation of the floor
repaired in the living room. You can see the basement

through the big hole. It is a 20 x20 room with a fireplace. We have an enormously heavy entertainment center that takes up almost the entire wall. It is extremely heavy, and they are not sure how to get it out. After much discussion, they decide to start cutting it up. This is about a $2,000 piece of furniture that is getting cut into pieces and thrown in the dumpster outside of our house. They could not pull the entertainment center because the hole was right in front of it and it would be too dangerous. The lightning hit the wall that the fireplace is on. There is a plug to the right of the fireplace, and the lightning hit that area and made a black mark on the wall. Once they removed the entertainment center, they began to repair the floor. We could not be in the house at the time of the repair because it was too dangerous.

When we came in and saw the 2 x 4's, we became very angry and frustrated. The boards were not lined up properly, and it appeared they installed used boards. There weren't enough nails on the floor to secure it. The wind bracing was supposed to be installed at a 45-degree angle, and the workers put them in straight across. We talked to the Contractor, and he said it was fine; it was no big deal. It was a big deal to Steve because we wanted the work done right and constructed the way our house was before the fire. The Construction Company is supposed to put your house exactly like it was before. Steve knows all about how the boards are to be installed and the proper bracing. It amazes me how much he knew about construction and the process. He has done many woodworking projects but building a house and a foundation that is secure; was something I did not realize he even knew. I am so grateful to Steve for his knowledge. He explained the process of building the house to the workers.

Unfortunately, most of them did not understand what he wanted. Our house is apparently not the standard house.

Workers are used to the houses that are all the same. (Our builder was a perfectionist, and that was one of the reasons we bought our home). Most of the time there were workers here doing the work, and there was one person here interpreting. It was hard at times because of the language barrier. Often the person in charge of the project would be there at the beginning and then leave. He was the Manager of the specific project and the only one who spoke English. The construction process was not going well at this point, and we started to realize the struggles we were going to face with this company and the communication issues. Most people do not know about the construction process and are not knowledgeable about what needs to be done but, Steve is very particular and is a perfectionist. He knew about how the wind bracing should be done and about the foundation. He knew the importance of getting the foundation on the main floor right. If it were not done right, the floors would squeak.

So, we met with other contractors to see if it would be a possibility to go with another company. It was a big job, and there was so much to be done. Both contractors we met, were a little apprehensive about starting a project that was started by another company. They gave us great suggestions, but we had to stick with the original contractors. We signed a contract with the current contractors, so we had to, at this point, keep them. We knew since this process did not go well; that we were going to face many challenges.

The foundation is what holds a house together. This was the main level of our house. It seems like a pretty simple process. You take board A and line up with board B to make a foundation. This reminded me of our Christian Life. The Christian walk is so simple. Believe and trust in God and do his will. We make it so complicated. We also build our house (our lives) on things that don't matter. Building a firm foundation is imperative in our lives and when building a house. It is important to stand firm on God's word; so, you won't be shaken. This process was not going to shake our family. We would stand on God's truths and His promises. Having faith that no matter what the circumstances that we would trust in Him.

The parable of the wise man and the foolish man is a good example. The wise man built his house upon a rock. The foolish man built his house upon the sand. When the rain came down, and the winds blew. The house on the rock did not fall but the house of the sand; it fell. This is like our lives; if we build our faith and hope in Christ, no storm will overtake us. If we build our hope in the world; then we will be broken. We, as a family, put our faith in God and we knew that He would put our lives together again.

Our family could not have gone through all that we had without having a foundation in Christ. Our home is in disrepair, right now, but we know with our God all things are possible. We are not trusting in a worldly man but a Godly Father. "My Grace is sufficient for you, for my strength is made perfect in weakness." During this time, we must seek God and draw on his strength, not ours.

The contractor has to tear out the boards and start some parts over. The boards were not the quality we had in our home before. Workers had put down cheaper boards, and Steve knew the difference. Steve made sure they put the boards in straight. He still did not manage to put enough nails in the floor, so Steve went around making sure the floor was secure. He began fixing the mistakes the workers had made. We as Christians; we make mistakes every day. It is important to ask for forgiveness and learn from our mistakes. It is time for us to forgive and to move on to the next step of building our home.

After the trouble with the construction framing process, I came to the house and prayed over it. I went to each room and prayed for the repairing of our home. I cried out to God and asked him to help us with the process. I learned that when faced with adversity and trials to cry out to God and really talk to him about your concerns. He hears and answers our prayers.

Even though the construction process is not going well at this point, we continue with our charity events. We are with an organization called the 501st, and it raises money for different charities. One of our first Charity Events was for a local parade. 501st had a big announcement, and we were honored to be a part of it. The Make A Wish Foundation was partnering with the 501st. This is the day we also got to meet Corey Dee and some of the puppeteers for BB8. They signed the inside of Steve's R2D2. This made his day! He was so excited and honored that they would take their time to sign his R2D2!! There were other R2D2's there that day, but he was the only one who got his signed. We were very thrilled to be a part of such a great organization. We are honored to think of others by participating in these troops, and we get to raise money for different charities.

We also went to a birthday party for a little boy with the 501st. The joy on the kids' faces made everything worthwhile. After that, we attended the ALS walk for Lou Gehrig's disease. We had a friend pass away from this many years ago, and this is an annual event for us. Chip asked us to come watch a Star Wars movie at the Church for his daughter's birthday. Ashley came as Rey, Tim as Han, Peanut as a Snow Trooper and R2D2. The kids had a great time watching the movie and hanging out with characters.

We attended a huge local church for their sermon on the Star Wars movie. At these events, we are all keeping a very positive attitude. We are telling others about our story and how God saved us from the fire. We did several other charity events; life for us went on as usual. We all came together and did what it took to think of others better than our ourselves. Not to focus on us during this season but to focus on people. "Do nothing out of selfish ambition or vain conceit. Rather in humility value others above yourselves. Not looking to your own interests but the each of you to the interests of others." Philippians 2:3-4 NIV. God reminded me of this verse and to always, during this process, to think of others better than myself.

The foundation of our home has been repaired, and Steve had to put a lot of nails in to secure it. The Wind stripping has been installed at a 45-degree angle in the living room and the office. Some of the sidings had to be replaced because of the fire. When you were in the basement, you could see the outside of the house. Boards were not lined up properly, so they had to redo this project as well. It took them awhile to get this process correct, but thankfully the foundation and the siding are now done.

We have all learned so much from this process. We are so glad that we have a foundation that is built on Jesus Christ. We are all so blessed to have him guiding and walking us through this process. We are so grateful that the foundation is secure. We are grateful that we have a good foundation in our home. We have had many challenges but so do we in life. It is how we handle these challenges that truly helps us realize how much trust we have in God.

Journal Entry:
Today, I evaluate my heart. It is mixed with different emotions. I find myself asking, "Why?" Why did we have to go through all the difficulties with the beginning of building our house? Why are there so many problems? Why do workers not understand simple instructions? All of us get angry at times. Especially during this season of trials. However, we did not take our anger out on workers. We prayed about each situation, and we tried to follow through in a Godly way. This is a time of fully seeking God. This began our process of fully relying on him. Our house will be completing someday, but it will be in his timing. Help me to find joy in our circumstances and to learn what you have for us in this process.

CHAPTER FIVE
Spirit is Overwhelmed
Getting out of the Pit

"LORD, hear my prayer,
listen to my cry for mercy;
in your faithfulness and righteousness
come to my relief.
Do not bring your servant into judgment,
for no one living is righteous before you.
The enemy pursues me,
he crushes me to the ground;
he makes me dwell in the darkness
like those long dead.
So my spirit grows faint within me;
my heart within me is dismayed.
I remember the days of long ago;
I meditate on all your works
and consider what your hands have done.
I spread out my hands to you;
I thirst for you like a parched land.
Answer me quickly, LORD;
my spirit fails.
Do not hide your face from me
or I will be like those who go down to the pit.
Let the morning bring me word of your unfailing love,
for I have put my trust in you.
Show me the way I should go,
for to you I entrust my life.
Rescue me from my enemies, LORD,
for I hide myself in you.

Teach me to do your will,
for you are my God;
may your good Spirit
lead me on level ground.
For your name's sake, LORD, preserve my life;
in your righteousness, bring me out of trouble.
In your unfailing love, silence my enemies;
destroy all my foes,
for I am your servant."
Psalm 143 (NIV)

We keep having major setbacks with the house. Our date to be back in the house was 2-12-17. Six months later. Due to starting late and many obstacles along the way the house will not be ready. Our official move out day is March 12th, and it looks like we must extend it out until April.

I am reminded that our comfort and my help comes from the Lord in Psalm 77 and also, I am reminded of Psalms 27, "The Lord is my shield my heart trusted in him, and I am helped therefore my heart greatly rejoices, and with my song, I will praise him." The song that has really helped me is called the Eye of the Storm. Just did not realize I was going to live out all of the lyrics. I sing this song a lot when times get tough.

Still having a hard time but I keep filling my head with scripture. Trying to get my stinkin' thinkin' gone and fill it with God's truth. On 1-13-17, another storm came our way. Steve lost his job with a company he had worked with for 19 years. He was given a two-week notice, so on 1-27-17, it would officially be his last day. Steve and I had no idea or indication this would happen. We were completely shocked!

See his boss loved his work and relied on him heavily. She called that day, and I happen to be in the bedroom where he worked, and she was on speaker phone. She had such a hard time telling him that the company was doing cut backs and that his position was no longer needed. She told him that a lot of people were losing their job that day. She told him that he would have a severance package. He would lose his insurance at the end of the month. How are we going to manage? I haven't worked in years because I stayed home with Ashley. I haven't had any experience working in over nine years. I graduated as a Medical Assistant many years ago, but I haven't worked in the field in 20 years.

Steve starts trying to get a resume ready and hired a company to help him. We had a lot of people asking for his resume, and he sent it out to so many people. He has not gotten any leads on any jobs. He tells me that he has been home with Ashley and I for so long that he doesn't want to lose his time with us. If he gets a job, he might have to travel or commute to work. Because he worked from home, he never had to drive anywhere. He really wants to focus on getting the house repaired. Everything at the house runs much smoother when Steve is there. Thankfully we just got our annual distribution check in December from his parents, so this should hold us for a while. We get a disbursement check each year from their retirement after they both passed away.

So, I started applying for jobs on online for a Nanny position. I got a callback and had an interview on the phone. After the interview, they asked me to meet them and their daughter. We all seemed to really like each other, but it was hard for all of us to trust each other immediately. Their baby was a preemie, so there were extra steps they took in taking care of her. They both agreed that I could come for a trial period to see how the baby liked me. They still wanted to try me out for several weeks to see if I am a good fit. All their food for the baby is homemade, and then they freeze it. They heat it up each time. This process is from a Dr. who lived to be 100. The babies that she took care of were very healthy. Ashley saw her when she was little, so we had that in common as well. They wanted to make sure I knew the process and the babies schedule. They put the baby on a schedule which keeps her much happier. Because she was a preemie, they also have a monitor that they put on her foot to make sure she is breathing. They also wanted me to keep track of the diapers and whether they are wet or dirty. I am so excited that God has placed this amazing family in my life. I was trying to decide what I would do after Ashley graduated and this is perfect!! I love babies, and I am so grateful for this amazing opportunity!! Praying they will like me and trust me during this trial period.

During this time, we also find out that Melayne's cancer is getting worse. She has only months to live. It is so hard because this is a time we would love to spend with her but with the fire and now working; there is not much time. We did get the opportunity to see her at Thanksgiving and have a wonderful meal with family. R2 even came to the dinner and sat at the table. She wanted Thanksgiving to be perfect. She had specific dishes she wanted to use and had the dinner planned perfectly. This was a hard and emotional time for everyone because we knew this would probably be her last meal with her family.

We had another trial that we were not expecting. Ashley is still dealing with issues from the concussion and has a hard time in loud situations. Sometimes when we do troops, she has to take time out to just sit and be quiet. She ended up quitting her job at the fast-food restaurant and started working full time for a hotel. She was also working at the church as a worship leader for the children's ministry all at the same time. She had two jobs and working on the Children's ministry. Until one day, she gets a text, not a phone call saying that she could take a break. We all had an enormous amount that we were all dealing with. We completely understood that this would probably be better for the church. This hurt Ashley deeply because she assumed she was being fired. She assumed that she was not doing a good job and completely started to shut down.

None of us wanted to go to church anymore because we did not understand why she was asked to take a break. She was told she could take a break and worship with her family. It took several months for us all to come together to talk. He allowed her to take a break because of the things we had going on in our lives. He was allowing Ashley time to heal and giving her the time to see her aunt.

We live in a texting and email generation. Words can be misinterpreted from email and texts. We could have prevented months of hurt from simply talking to him versus texting each other. We knew his heart and knew that he would never hurt Ashley on purpose. It took time to restore and strengthen our friendship because we didn't simply just talk. Talking to each other develops true Christian friendships that will last a lifetime.

Several weeks prior we had just had a meeting with him and the Pastor. Telling them our struggles and how we were really hurting because Steve lost his job, the house fire and we told him Melayne was really sick. We talked about how people had not reached out to us. Steve was on the tech team, Ashley and I sang in the choir, and I was also on the coffee team. People would ask how we were doing if they saw us at Church. I am not sure they knew what to do or how to help us. Steve and I have been through so many trials and that we as a couple just rely on each other and God.

We went to see the Pastor because of Ashley. She told us she didn't see the point in life. She thought that so many bad things keep happening to us and she did not want Tim to have to endure all of this. She was struggling with her faith and didn't understand why bad things happen to good people. We talked with the Pastor, but he offered her to see a counselor. A counselor? A counselor would cost money. We don't have much money because Steve does not have a job. So, I began earnestly praying for her and encouraged her to get in the word. This was slowly starting to help her feel better, and then she gets asked not to come back for children's ministry. Our hearts are all so broken. So hurt. But we know that God is in control, and we must keep our faith.

When your spirit is overwhelmed, and you are heartbroken, our Father promises to be close to you during this time. Psalm 34:18-19 NIV. Lord Help me to forgive and know that this happened for a reason. We are supposed to pray God's will. I am having a hard time praying much less praying for his will. There is so much in our lives right now that are overwhelming us. I am just not sure how to pray. How do you pray when your heart is hurting and so emotional? I am starting to pray the scriptures, especially in Psalms. David seems to know exactly how I feel. How do you pray when you are faced with so much? This is a song Ashley, and I wrote:

Can you Hear Me Now?
Can you Hear my prayer?
I feel like there's no one there.
I am praying that you hear me
I am hoping you can see me
I am begging you to please speak to me now
Can you hear me now?

Journal Entry:
Praying God will deliver me out of the pit that I am in spiritually, physically and mentally. Pray as our circumstances begin to change. For I pray that we are forever changed because of the fire and the storms we have been through. I relate so much to David in the pit. The crying for help from God. I find hope that God heard David's prayers and He hears mine.

Now is a time to forgive and to work together as a family like we always do. Working together, praying and seeking the Lord is the only way to make it through the storms in life. Each storm is different but requires that you are faithful and trust that God will bring you through the waves of life.

Hebrew 12:6 NIV He disciplines the one he loves and chastens everyone He accepts as His own. Endure hardship and discipline; God is treating you as His children. For what children are not disciplined by their Father. Verse 10, God disciplines us for your good in order that we might share His holiness. No discipline seems pleasant at the time but painful. Later on, however, it produces a harvest of righteousness and peace for all who have been trained by it.

Eye of the storm has encouraged me through this season. Tonight, as I am driving to pick up Ashley, there is lightning all around me. So, I called my Mom and asked her to pray, and then I hang up immediately; crying on the phone. Off to my right, there is a red area, and at first, it looked like it might be from sirens. Then the clouds began to get darker, and the lightning got so much worse. I could not see the car in front of me. I am at Exit 111, and 109 is the exit to get Ashley. 2 miles. Then suddenly, you see a spiral, which appeared to be a tornado off to the right, not sirens. I was headed directly in the eye of the storm. I have the radio on, it is playing, "I am Going Home." I screamed," God I don't want to go home. I don't want to die tonight!" I truly thought that this was the end of my life. I thought of Melayne and how she was battling cancer, and I thought I would get to Heaven before her. I want to see Ashley get married and grow up. I want to see my family. So, I turn the radio off and start screaming, literally. 'In the eye of the storm, you remain in control, in the middle of the war, you guard my soul, you alone are the anchor, when my sails are torn, your love surrounds me in the eye of the storm.' The lightning and the storm is getting worse. I start screaming God you are faithful. Thank you for loving me. I know you are going to carry me through this storm. Just like it says it Mark, "Speak to the mountain and it will move." The clouds and the lightning started calming down. I was at my exit. God allowed me to pass through the storm and thankfully He let me live.

Even though in this season, this storm had to be the hardest, I know that God hears my prayers and will walk with me through these storms. I pray that Ashley and Steve will know this as well. God should never be your last resort in life. He should be the first person we seek when faced with adversity. This is a season of getting to know my God even better. My Father who created me. I will always be eternally grateful for this season of pain and knowing he will carry me through the storm.

When faced with storms in life, you must have faith. Faith that God hears your prayers. Faith that he will bring you through it. That no matter how bad the circumstances are that you know God will take care of you. Keep your eyes on God; not on your circumstances. Praise God in the storms of life! Praise His goodness and faithfulness! He is God of mercy and forgiveness! So glad He hears my prayers and is so faithful to all of us! Psalm 34:1 KJV, "I will bless the Lord at all times: his praise shall continually be in my mouth." I am also encouraged by Psalm 34:17 KJV, "The righteous cry and the Lord heareth and delivereth them out of their troubles. The Lord is near unto them that are of a broken heart. Many are the afflictions of the righteous, but the Lord delivered him out of them all." Praise God He hears our prayers and will deliver us all throughout the storms in life. So, looking forward to what God can do!

The only person who shows up to a pity party is the devil; one local Pastor declares. God promises to take care of us. I can't focus on my circumstances now just because they look bad and overwhelming. It is time for our family to focus on God. It is important to praise God in the mountaintops of life and in the valleys. Reminding ourselves of what He has brought us through and to. What He brings you to; He will equip to bring you through! Thank God, we all don't look like what we have been through. God delivers us all!

When you are going through a dark time in your life, focus on what you have, to be thankful for. Praise God for His truth and promises. He is a God worthy to be praised. Circumstances may not go the way you planned them but God, most of the time, has a bigger plan. Joy is a sign of a healthy Christian. As it says in James, "Count it ALL joy when you face trials of various kinds." ESV. It is important to be thankful for everything, just as Paul, be joyful. "A heart of peace gives life to the body, but envy rots the bones."

Journal Entry:
God may not take our burdens away, but he will walk us through it to teach us what he wants us to learn. God promises to remain by our side. Psalm 23:4

Psalm 138:7-8 Though I walk in the midst of trouble you REVIVE me!! You have stretched out your hand against my enemies. You have perfected the things that concerned me. Your mercy has endured through this trial. Thank you for bringing us through the storms of life.

Psalm 34:18 The Lord is close to the brokenhearted and saves those who are crushed in spirit.

1Peter 3:17 For it is better, if it is God's will, to suffer for doing good than for doing evil.

Psalm 55:16-17 I will call upon God, and the Lord shall save me. Evening, Morning and at noon. I will pray and cry aloud and hear my voice.

Journal Entry and Prayer:

This is a time that is hard to pray. I am reminded today that you hear our prayers, and I should pray often. Lack of prayer means losing ground to the enemy. Our role is to pray. We are to speak God's word in love and believe that God will cast down strongholds. Listen to God's truth.

Prayer is not to manipulate God but to bring transformation to your heart. Prayer is ongoing communication. Prayer is a pouring out to God letting him know your true feelings. I have often prayed his words because the Psalms have really expressed the feelings that have been in my heart.

Prayer during this season is simply Lord forgive me for not praying. It is so hard to pray when I feel so broken and displaced. You have been with us every step and through every storm. Feels like I am in a weird place emotionally and spiritually. Please help me not to take for granted the power of prayer. Give me a passion for seeking the lost. Help me to speak words of wisdom and encourage others. Thank you for helping me share this story. Thank you for the courage you give me daily.

CHAPTER SIX
A Season of Waiting

Wait for the Lord; be strong and take heart
and wait for the Lord.
Psalm 27:14 (NIV)

Today I am sitting in the waiting room at the hospital. Waiting for Doctors to find out the cause of my Mother's bleeding. Waiting on the outcome can be stressful, but I choose to trust in God through it.

Waiting for Steve to start trying to find a job and waiting for him to get a job. Steve told us that he had been home with Ashley and I for 20 years. He has always worked from home. He is scared that if he finds a job, it is going to take him away from his family. He doesn't want to travel. He is also concerned that he would have a long distance to get to work. He would not have the flexibility that he has had in the past. Also, he feels that he would not be able to do the charity work with R2. I am so grateful that I have a husband that wants to be around and really cherishes his family.

Waiting, today, to see how Melayne's cancer is doing. She is having scans today to see if chemo and radiation is working. Waiting, today, to find out whether my Brother's foster kids will be staying with them. My brother has five foster kids. Two have been adopted. They are required to attend court days all the time. They show up to court and then sometimes the Judge extends a decision for another month. We have all gotten so attached to all the kids. Praying that the kids will be able to stay with Harvey and Jean. The kids have truly been a blessing!!

Today is also the day that we find out what Tim (Ashley's boyfriend) is allergic to. Tim had a very severe reaction to something he ate, and the Doctors are running allergy testing.

I am also waiting to find out if I get the Nanny job permanently. God has given me the opportunity to possibly care for a family as a Nanny. I love taking care of kids, and I pray that I can be a blessing to the right family. Praying that I wait for the right family and the one God has for me. Today has been a huge day in prayer and seeking God. My Mother's bleeding was nothing serious and can be taken care of with medication. The Inspection did not pass, on the house, because the wires from the street are 2 inches short. This will take a few days to get the proper wires required. Steve will be getting unemployment and did not look for a job today, but I know he will. I know God will supply all our needs. I know God is faithful and that we can manage, with God's help. My Brother's two babies get to stay!! We are all so excited!! Hoping and praying that someday we can be their forever family.

Melayne's cancer is worse, and it has spread. You can visibly see tumors on her neck. She does not have much time with us. We are dealing with so much with the house, that we have not been able to take time to spend with her. We realize now that we need to spend some quality time with her. We do know, however, that she believes in Jesus and has asked for forgiveness. She just recently started attending Church and learning more about him. She will be going to Heaven soon, and it is so hard to accept that. We found out today that Tim is allergic to garlic, paprika, and peppers. I feel bad for him because he loves all these foods so much. His face, eyes, and tongue would begin to swell, so he has had to stay away from all of those spices.

I found out that I got the job a few days later. So, thankful for this amazing opportunity!! I arrived at the house, and I knew their Housekeeper. Her son was in the same class as Ashley in 4th grade. Her Mother came over later, and she was a Teacher at the school where my daughter attended. Wow! I knew that God had placed me with the right family. I am so excited about this opportunity!! Since Steve had not found a job, being a Nanny, was a job I was able to get quickly to help my family out. I am so grateful and cannot wait to start taking care of the baby!! Steve will be getting unemployment. I know God will supply all our needs. God is supplying our needs financially in ways we could have never imagined. We got a distribution check, severance package, and some insurance money.

Obedience and faith mean leaving the consequences to God. I am to trust God through this fire and through these storms in life. I am not to have any fear, but faith only! God challenges us during these times to fully rely on Him and trust Him through the storms. Some situations did not go the way we hoped, but we must trust God even though we don't understand. He is a God that sees the whole picture and the whole story. Trusting and keeping our faith is the only way to get through the storms in life. Trials are still going to come but trusting in Him makes it a lot easier. Our faith in Jesus makes us safe in the Lord's care.

Journal Entry:

Praying today that as our circumstances change we also will change because of the storms in life. Praying today that our lives will not go back to "normal" but our lives will forever be impacted because of this season. In every season, in every circumstance, "This Too Shall Pass." This was one of the scriptures I would often focus on during the storms in life.

Proverbs 14:30 NIV God give us His peace to go through trials. Not as the world gives but as He gives. Trust in His peace and promises this too shall pass. This season will pass, and God will walk you through the other storms in life.

Journal Entry 1-30-17

Spirit is overwhelmed, but I am reminded of Psalm 77 that comfort comes from God. I am reminded to remember the works of the Lord and what He has done for us. I will meditate of the good work and talk of the doings vs. 2 KJV Psalm 78:7 ESV to set your hope in God and keep His commandments. God loves His people! My help comes from the Lord! I cry out to you today from the depths of my soul. Psalm 28:7, The Lord is my shield, my heart trusted in him, and I am helped therefor my heart greatly rejoices, and with my song, I will praise him!!

I lift up my eyes to the mountains—
 Where does my help come from?
My help comes from the Lord,
 the Maker of heaven and earth.
Psalm 121:1-2 (NIV)

Psalm 27:1-4 Whom shall I fear? The lord is the strong hold of my life. When the wicked advance against me it is my enemies and my foes who will stumble and fall. One thing I ask from the Lord that I dwell in the house of the Lord forever. For in the days of trouble he will keep me safe in his dwelling. Hear my voice when I call Lord: Be merciful to me and answer me. Teach me your way, Lord. Lead me in a straight path because of my oppressors.

Journal Entry:
Psalm 130:5 I wait for the Lord; my soul waits and in his word I hope. Have you ever been in a season of waiting? Waiting on the outcome of things that are out of your control. Waiting on Doctors and Nurses to give you the results. Waiting is hard sometimes, especially when you don't know the outcome.

2-1-17 - A Day of waiting on God. Today, I wait for the inspections to be done for the electric. They cannot move forward with any more construction until the electric has passed inspection. Drywall should start tomorrow if inspections pass. The Inspector has come out twice without informing anyone. Therefore, no one was there to let him in to inspect the property. Today we wait, hoping and praying, that this final inspection will pass. We know that all things will come together in HIS timing, not ours. Thankful for the process!

David teaches us to wait for God's timing and the danger of moving ahead with our plans. When we move ahead in life without God, we can make a mess out of our lives and miss out on God's great plans. Waiting and listening for God's plan will help many blessings come your way.

CHAPTER SEVEN
Wasting Time

Teach us to number our days,
that we may gain a heart of wisdom.
May the favor of the Lord our God rest on us;
establish the work of our hands for us—
yes, establish the work of our hands.
Psalm 90:12 (NIV)

Workers have wasted a lot of time and energy with the house and the projects. If they would just take their time and think about what they are doing it would save them time and money. Each project had to be redone, as all the projects in the house, never were it done right the first time. The only exception, was the carpet, for which we found a local company, for the installation. Some projects had to be re-done several times. Some projects began as fixing something and destroying something else. This has been a time of many obstacles and many challenges. I realized it takes time for God to mold us into the people He wants us to be. He tries to fix us, and then we mess up with the choices we make. It will take time for our house to be completed but it will be in His perfect timing. He is 'all-knowing,' and He knows what is best for us. He is teaching us so much through these storms in our lives. I know that He has a great plan for our lives and He will use this storm for His glory.

I could use this time of waiting and waste time or choose to spend it on reading God's word and getting closer to him. I choose to write this book hoping that it will encourage the lives of others. If God impacts one person with our story, it will be worth it. I also write because God has told me to and in those times of wasting time; I can use it as productive time. I try to write each day about what God has taught me. I write the emotions and feelings. I write out my prayers because it is so good to see when they are answered!! How much time do we spend a day wasting time? The things we do in life, are they really going to matter for the Kingdom? Are we spending our time on things that really make a difference in the world?

I am in a season of going through the motions at times. I spend time on Facebook looking at others' lives. I spend a lot of time reading emails. I love doing these 'things,' but I need to make sure to spend time with God and learn more about him. It is in these quiet times I should be learning and reading God's word. Preparing for the next season and the next storm.

In James, the Bible says that we will face trials. James 1:2-4 NIV "Consider it pure joy my brothers and sisters, whenever you face trials of many kinds because you know that the testing of your faith produces perseverance. Let perseverance finish its work so that you may be mature and complete lacking in nothing."

Spending time with God in prayer. Making each day count and counting everything a joy!! Each day is a gift from God. We never know when our time on earth will end. Spending time in prayer is important. Again, praying is not to manipulate God, but it is to bring transformation to your heart. Prayer is ongoing communication with God. I talk to God about everything, and I have seen some tremendous miracles in my life. I want to make sure I am focusing on things that matter and make my life a living example for

Christ. Today has been a HUGE day in prayer and seeking God!!

Journal Entry:
Psalm 39:4-5 NLT "LORD, remind me how brief my time on earth will be. Remind me that my days are numbered–how fleeting my life is. You have made my life no longer than the width of my hand. My entire lifetime is just a moment to you; at best, each of us is but a breath."

Colossians 3:23-24 (NIV) Whatever you do, work at it with all your heart, as working for the Lord, not for human masters, since you know that you will receive an inheritance from the Lord as a reward. It is the Lord Christ you are serving.

God revealed to me in this season of waiting that I am pouring my love into the baby I nanny for. It may not seem significant to many people, but to me, I am honored that he chose me to take care and to help this precious child at such an impressionable age. Thank you for the realization, God!!

Everyone wants to live a life of significance. Leaving an impact unto the world is a goal that is important to me. Melayne will leave such a legacy as a Professor, Mother and a Wife. Her legacy will carry on with her students that she taught in college. What can you do to have a long-lasting impact on the world? How about loving people because God made them? Love ALL people. We can only make a difference, if we allow God to work through us, in our lives.

Spread His word to everyone you meet. Make God the center of your life. Be consumed with Him. When we focus on Him; He will help us love and be kind to others. God, I'm living life through the storm.

Ps 37:4 NIV Delight yourself in the Lord and he will give you the desires of your heart.

CHAPTER EIGHT
Floors and Carpets

The LORD is close to the brokenhearted
and saves those who are crushed in spirit.
Psalm 34:18 (NIV)

So, since the process of the house has been challenging,
Steve and I decide that we are going to get our own
contractor, for the hardwoods and carpets. We go to meet
with a Mom and Pop Store that we had used when we
finished the basement back in 2009. We went to the store
and picked out a light color for the upstairs and bedrooms
and the stairs. I thought the stairs would get to be hardwood,
but it was going to be too much and very expensive to make
it look right. I was a little disappointed because the carpets
get so dirty on the stairs. We are so fortunate that we are
getting some things done differently as we are repairing our
home. One thing that is different, for sure, is that we are
choosing hardwood floors to go on the main level. We decide
on a light wood with wider boards. The Mom and Pop Shop
will take care of hardwoods, carpet, vinyl in the laundry
room and tile in hall in basement.

We had builder grade carpet in our house before, so we
pick out a little nicer carpet, with a thicker pad for the
upstairs area. We have a dog, so we wanted to get carpet with
a pet stain resistant. We choose a darker beige for the
downstairs in the basement. We were a little disappointed
because they did not have the carpet we originally had in the
basement. We picked out the Stain master carpet with a very
nice pad. We are upgrading the carpet and the hardwood

floors on the main level. We were told that we might have to pay some more money at the end of the process, but Steve and I wanted our house to be changed, just as I know our lives will be changed from this process.

We finished our basement back in 2009 after Steve's parents passed away. Building the basement was a healing process for him. He put all his emotion into building a beautiful room. It is a 20 x 20 room and in the front of the room he built an area so he could get to the wires of the media room. We had a concrete area so Steve chooses to build a shelf around it so he could access wiring. He built a trey ceiling around the whole room with crown molding on it to finish. He had black ceiling tiles with what appeared to be stars. They were actually straight pins, dipped in fluorescent paint and individually put into the ceiling tiles. He had a light that turned on the stars. Each area of the room he designed and built to his specifications. He had a cabinet, with all the electronic equipment, neatly organized.

In 2017, as the construction workers begin to try to rebuild the basement; it is not going well. They tried to build the trey ceiling, and it was not level. It was a box as opposed to a trey. It was also not supported properly and would not carry the weight. So, the project was going to have to start over. This is an ongoing theme for rebuilding our house. Steve tried so hard to talk to them about the process and how he wanted it built. He drew a picture with dimensions, but they did not understand what he wanted. He even contacted the original contractor to try to help him build it, but he did not have time to help him. So, Steve decided to build the trey ceiling himself. He designed the trey ceiling with his own original design. He began prepping and making each part of the ceiling. The boards had to be cut to a specific length. Everything had to be measured and cut with precision. Most of the contractors never measured. They all seemed to nail it in place and never measure for accuracy. Steve is a perfectionist, and if a ¼ of an inch is off, it is not right and rightly so.

Building the trey ceiling for him is once again a healing process. You see, his sister has taken a turn for the worse. Hospice has been called in. She has quit her job as a Professor. She now has a hospital bed. Hard to cope with; that she will be gone soon.

Steve deals with his emotions and difficulties in projects. This is his way of coping with life situations. Melayne is his only sibling, and his parents have been gone since 2009. This room reflects the outpouring of emotions that he felt with his parents and now his sister. The contractor could not understand why this room of all the rooms in the house was so important to him. I talked to him privately, and then he began to understand.

Steve gets the trey ceiling built, and the contractors are going to install it. We have 12-foot ceilings in the basement, so they had to have ladders. Steve and I are not here when they install it or when they work on the cabinet around the cement blocks. We come in, and the trey ceiling is not level. We call the contractor and have him look at it, and he says he didn't see anything wrong with it. Steve said, "Look at that trey ceiling it is off a ½ inch and is not level." They got a measuring tape and measured, and the trey ceiling was exactly ½ inch off. So, they have to take the nails and screws out and move it down exactly a ½ inch.

The contractors tried to make the shelving around the cement blocks. The trey ceiling and shelves are carpentry work involving precise measurements. Contractors are used to making houses all the same with no special designs. Our house was full of special projects for which Steve had designed and engineered. If we had your basic house, these projects would have gone so much smoother. But, because Steve was an engineer, full of imagination and skills, our house was much harder to repair. So, Steve ended up building the shelves around the cement. This time he built a shelving around the cement but left an area open for storing movies and games. The top would open, and he could access any of the wirings if he needed to. The cabinet and shelf were so beautiful. He is an amazing engineer and carpenter. The contractor could not believe his level of expertise.

These workers do this work every day, and they struggled to get this job done. Steve put this all together in a matter of days, and it was absolutely perfect!! The contractor said, 'it was beautiful, but my guys don't have the time to spend on a project like that. They will do projects that are standard but a carpenter should have been called in for this project.' It got to be a joke with Steve and I when the contractor needed something done. Hosea the painter would get called in; he tried to install the attic fan, and they had to get a roofer. Hosea was great at painting and odd jobs but not at everything. He was called for many jobs that he had no idea what he was doing. Such as the basement and creating the trey ceiling.

The floors are getting acclimated to the house and carpets are getting installed! To put the carpets in the installers, the natural light from outside must be used. But we still do not have lights in the house. We are still having a hard time getting the permit. The carpets go in upstairs with no problems. They put plastic on the carpets in the walking areas so that they would not get messed up. We still have contractors, and we will eventually have movers in the house. The carpet is very light, and we are hoping and praying it does not get messed up. It looks so beautiful!! Our home is starting to come together, but we still have no light. How many years have we all been through a dark place in our lives with no light? It seems as if the light will never shine again. We are starting to get discouraged about the light but knows that God will shine his light on our lives in the right timing.

Today we meet the floor guy to install the floors to pick out colors. He comes and tries to match the color of the stairs. We talk about advantages of having a light color versus dark. Every color he mixes is either too dark or too light. He mixes several colors together and comes up with a color that is beautiful. He is a very experienced hardwood floor guy. We are very pleased with his work.

He brings in the boards to cure to the house for about a week. Once he installs the floor, no one can walk on the floors for a few days. Finally, we will get a break with the house and can go see Melayne. If no one is in the house, we don't have workers to manage. Every time we have left workers alone the project did not go as planned or discussed. Each project Steve has had to give specific instructions and specific measurements. It is hard for them to understand and to measure anything during this construction process.

We decide that we will go see Melayne's over the weekend. No one is supposed to be in the house. We have a sign on the door in English and Spanish. Melayne lives in

Columbia, South Carolina, so it will be about a 4-hour drive. We are shocked when we arrive. She has tumors on her neck that are visible. Steve, Ashley and I are still holding on to faith that God could heal her. We had a great time talking and hanging out. We made plans for the next few weeks to care for her. I made a schedule for her to eat and take her meds. I encouraged her to get up out of bed, and she could watch a movie with us. It was hard for us all to imagine that she was so sick and we had so much going on with the house. We wanted to be here with her all the time. I have to work every week, but I took off, to spend this time with her. She wanted people to come one at a time as opposed to a big group. So grateful that we could spend quality time together. We scheduled her In-laws to be the next family to visit. We had paid for a trip to Orlando for a big Convention. Melayne really wanted us to go. It was extremely emotional to leave her that day. We knew at the time it might be the last time we see her.

Steve, Ashley and I have been preparing for a Celebration event for quite some time. It was going to be our break from house stuff and time away that we desperately needed. Melayne had family coming in, so we felt like she would be fine, while we were away. But just before we left she called me; to tell me that she would not be here in a few weeks. She asked if her Aunts that were scheduled at the end of the month could come now. Aunt Marylin, Susan, and Dode got flights out a few days later, and they could take care of Melayne during this time.

Melayne wanted us to go on our trip. She wanted to hear the fun things we were doing and so we Face=timed with her. The day we left, we drove all the way to Florida, overnight.

Arrived around 7:30 am. Steve got us tickets to the Magic Kingdom, and off we went to the parks. We had so much fun hanging out at Disney and enjoying this precious time as a family. We sent Melayne pictures every day. We called her to see how she was doing. Each day she got a little weaker. We all felt so bad for being there, knowing she was sick and fighting for her life. But, she wanted to see her Aunts and for us to go on vacation.

The celebration was filled with lots of characters from the movie Star Wars. The 501st had a room full of costumes. There were people walking around in costumes. Also, there was an exhibit room with props from the movie. I am not a huge Star Wars fan, but this was pretty cool!! They also had a droid room full of R2D2's, BB8 and Choppers. Each day they would have a parade at two o'clock. It was so fun to see the droids in the parade each day. On Friday, all of the droids were lining up to get a picture. It was taking a long time. I get a FACETIME call from Melayne. Susan says Melayne wants to talk to you now. Ashley did not get to see Melayne before we left. She was always working. Melayne said, "Let me see my beautiful niece." So, Ashley and I moved over to a quiet area and talked to Melayne. Then she asked to speak with Steve. He was getting ready for the parade so I asked Susan if he could call her back. She said, "No he needs to talk with her now." So, I ask Steve to talk with her, and he ends up on Facetime with his sister. We were all sad because we thought this might be the last time we got to talk with her. We all knew the time was drawing near for her. We ask if she wanted us to come home and she said to stay and enjoy.

On the way back from Florida, we all want to get home, because we know Melayne's time is short. We actually leave a day early. On the way home, there is a black car that is weaving in and out of traffic. It appears that the person is drunk or driving very badly. I ask Steve to back off from the car. We are following this car for miles, and it seems like his driving is getting much worse. I ask Steve to really slow down so this person can get way ahead of us. Moments later we see a car skidding off the road. The cars in front of us are putting on their brakes. We are behind a semi. The Semi turns his truck to the left right in front of us. Steve applies the brakes, and the anti-lock brakes end up stopping, and our car is inches away from the semi. The semi drives away but up ahead we see a dark car in the middle of the interstate, and we see a car on the side of the road.

We pulled our car over to see if someone needed help. The car off to the right of us spun and hit a tree going at least 65 miles an hour. I am praying before the accident happened for God to protect the driver. We walk up to the car, and the woman is walking out of her car. Wait she just hit a tree going 65 miles an hour, and she walked out of her car. She was so concerned about her car being totaled; not sure how she was going to pay for it. I told her that God saved and protected her and He would walk with her every step of the way. The car that was weaving was in the middle of the intersection. We saw two kids running out of the car. It was a hit and run. Once again, God showed us his amazing power to protect us all!! We all could have died that day and the people in the accident. It was that close and that scary for all of us. But, when I saw the car weaving, the first thing I did, was pray. Pray for God's protection. How was no one hurt? God is the only explanation. You don't usually walk away from accidents like this.

We got the call that Steve's sister would probably not make it much longer. We drove home to Atlanta and Steve drove to South Carolina. He made it in time to see her. She smiled at him. She was very peaceful now. She passed away on Thursday 4/20/2017. An important lesson we learned; is to cherish the time you have with people; especially your loved ones. You never know when it will be your last time seeing them. Always let people know your true feelings for each other because you never know when God will call them home. Melayne had stage 3 cancer. We never gave up hope. She was only 51 years old and had a beautiful child ten years old. She has been married for many years to Don. We are all mourning the loss of Melayne; a sister, a friend.

Melayne's funeral would be planned by her friends a week later. This would give us all time to process it and to face reality. She had a beautiful service with lots of friends and colleagues. She had a slide show with all of her family and friends. She had an open mic time when family and friends could come and speak about her. She had so many friends from growing up together. So many people cared about her!! Her funeral inspired me to leave the legacy she has left. We all have a hole in our heart from not having her here. But, she has taught us all so much, especially the "gift of love."

When we get back to the house, no one was supposed to be in it while we were gone. All the ceiling tiles for the basement was painted. The ceiling in the basement was put up with white ceiling tiles. The ceiling was not straight and level. They curved the ceiling to avoid the pipes. Steve was furious that they worked on the house without us being home.

Unfortunately, this has been the theme of the workers at the house. They needed constant management of each project. The carpets were the only projects that went as instructed. The ceiling tiles were painted with the wrong kind of paint which would cause the ceiling tiles to sag. Each tile was supposed to be laid out flat and painted with a certain paint. Each tile would need 4 to 5 coats of paint so that the white would not show through. They added more paint, but Steve will eventually have to fix it. The ceiling in the hall cannot be fixed. We will have a crooked ceiling in the hall. Everything was supposed to be put back exactly as it was. Workers are having a hard time, especially with the basement.

Today we have another major setback. We are all having a hard time understanding why these bad things keep happening. Why do the workers keep making mistakes? Why do they create more problems? That is like us as Christians. We make mistakes every day. We make the same mistakes and sometimes don't learn from our mistakes. Each day is a new day, and God forgives us. It is time for us to forgive the workers for their mistakes. Hoping and praying that we will all have our home again soon. It may not be exactly as our house was before but we are changed, and our house will always be a reminder of that change.

Our major setback was the cabinet guy came at 6:00 pm to install cabinets in the kitchen. He was rushing because he had a long day. He poked a hole in the pipe, but he did not notice it. Steve calls me and tells me there is water in the basement. I am at work and cannot really help. I called our friend John, and he came over right away. He could help Steve with the water in the basement. Then they come back upstairs, and in the kitchen, the floors are ruined. The kitchen has water all over the brand-new hardwood floors. The cabinet guy left. We called the contractor and let him know. He has to bring in new floors and let them cure for a week. All the cabinets must come back out, and the kitchen floors will need to be replaced. We are all so thankful that Steve and John were there to dry up the water and to take care of the damage the cabinet guy made. This situation could have been much worse if Steve was not there working in the basement. Steve worked on the house and on the cabinets, anything that would help us get back in the house sooner.

One of the problems with the workers now is that they are coming to our house, after a long day of work. They are arriving at 6 or 7 at night to start a job that takes several hours. Then they get tired, and the job does not get done, and then they make mistakes. So, we tell the Contractor that there is absolutely no one allowed to work after 6:00 and that we need to know when workers are here. It needs to be scheduled so that we can manage projects. We live in apartments about 30 minutes away; so, it takes time for us to get here. The contractor gave us a spreadsheet with plans for the next few months. This should have happened at the beginning of the project, yet we are grateful we have a plan moving forward.

We learned during this season to cherish the life God has given us. We never know when we will take our last breath. It is important to me to leave a legacy and to make an impact unto the world. To leave the world a better place. To share God's message with those around us. Getting God's message is more important to me than ever before. I realize the importance of having that everlasting relationship with God.

It takes time for God to mold us into the people He wants us to be. It will take time for our house to become our home again. We are completed in His perfect timing, and our house will be completed in His timing. He is "all knowing," and he knows what is best for us. We must trust him with whatever circumstances come our way. Storms will come in life, but it is imperative that you keep your faith through the storm.

Prov. 3:25-26 NIV Do not be afraid of sudden terror nor trouble from the wicked when it comes; for the Lord will be your confidence and will keep your foot from being caught.

We are having to constantly remind ourselves that God is in control. Every problem and every situation. We cannot have fear, but faith. Faith and trusting God is the only way we will get through this storm. He is our refuge and our strength in times of trouble. Fear causes us to miss out on the beauty and joy that exists in everyday life. God says, "Do not be afraid. Fear not I am with you."

Journal Entry:
Some people view obstacles as problems. The Lord can show himself through our problems. He can show his awesome power. If we view trials as trouble, then we can miss the demonstration of God's love, power, and wisdom.

Matthew 17:14-21 (NIV) When they came to the crowd, a man approached Jesus and knelt before him. "Lord, have mercy on my son," he said. "He has seizures and is suffering greatly. He often falls into the fire or into the water. I brought him to your disciples, but they could not heal him." "You unbelieving and perverse generation," Jesus replied, "how long shall I stay with you? How long shall I put up with you? Bring the boy here to me." Jesus rebuked the demon, and it came out of the boy, and he was healed at that moment. Then the disciples came to Jesus in private and asked, "Why couldn't we drive it out?" He replied, "Because you have so little faith. Truly I tell you, if you have faith as small as a mustard seed, you can say to this mountain, 'Move from here to there,' and it will move. Nothing will be impossible for you."

CHAPTER NINE
We have Light!

The LORD is my light and my salvation—
whom shall I fear?
The LORD is the stronghold of my life—
of whom shall I be afraid?
Psalm 27:1 (NIV)
Your word is a lamp for my feet,
a light on my path.
Psalm 119:105 (NIV)
I have hidden your word in my heart
that I might not sin against you
Psalm 119:11 (NIV)

2-9-17 Drywall is delivered to house. Steve and I just checked on the house this morning. But Steve felt in his spirit that he needed to check on the house again, so he drove back over. He looked at the drywall, and it was not the mold resistant drywall that we had before the fire. Steve and I tried to figure out what had happened. Was it the Contractor that told him the wrong drywall or did the workers pick up the wrong order? We finally get to the bottom of the problem. The person that loaded the drywall at the store loaded the wrong kind. The workers must then load up the wrong drywall which is very heavy and go back to the store and get the right kind.

Today my Bible Study was about Jonah running away from the Lord. Sometimes with these problems that would seem to be an easier solution; to run away. God has allowed these obstacles to test our faith. Are we going to stay faithful even when our circumstances get hard? Today is not a day to run away from God but run to him. God is so much bigger than these circumstances and trials we face. Praying today that we all don't run from God but focus on him instead of our trials.

After the drywall arrived, everything started moving quickly. The workers did a great job on the drywall and the whole process. The Contractor kept asking me to pick out paint colors. I had such a hard time, so I met with a Decorator, at the paint store. I did not want the colors we had before. I wanted a color that was different. I wanted a change when buying things for the house. All our lives had changed drastically, and we all wanted a house that showed change. The Decorator advised me on the paint colors that were popular. I choose what she picked out. The colors were a lot of blues and grays. When we tested out the color on the wall, it was too much! We are all simple, and it really did not fit our home or personalities. We had to go back to the store and start again. Steve and I have been to the paint store several times. He wants me to pick out the paint for the main floor and our bedrooms. The Contractor is asking me every day for the colors. It is so much pressure picking out colors when you are not sure what it will look like. I thought it would be fun to put color in the rooms. I had a green in our living room before the fire, but I wanted change. Our lives had changed, and I really wanted a new look. The painters are coming tomorrow, and they need the paint and the color. It is so much pressure to decide. Steve still hasn't gotten a job, so we are not sure if we might have to move. Is it smart to put color in the house if we may possibly need to sell the house? We all want to be comfortable and reflect change in our house, but we choose to make a change in other ways. Steve and I decided on a very light beige throughout the whole house. Steve is always the sensible one when making decisions. I wanted color, but it makes sense to add color to the room and not to the walls. I am so glad I can rely on his leadership and great choices for our family.

Painters come the next day and start painting. The color is going up everywhere, and it looks great! Steve and I love the color we chose. We do not have light at this point because we are still having a hard time getting power on. So, the painters are using a generator, and they brought lights in so they can paint.

Steve is also using a generator he bought to restore the cabinets downstairs in his workshop. His Grandpa helped him make handmade cabinets specific to his needs. During the demolition process, they wanted to demo the cabinets because they had fire damage all over them. Steve's Grandfather passed away many years ago, which is why these cabinets were so important to keep. While the reconstruction has been going on, they were in the garage. Now Steve is spending hours cleaning and restoring these priceless cabinets. It takes weeks of work, but he restored them and painted them beautifully.

The painters work each day with the generator and the huge lights. The first day the project was going very well. Then the painters ran out of paint. So, they get the code from the paint can, but they went to another location to get the paint. They came back and started painting. They painted the downstairs hallway and bathroom with the new paint. Steve and I come to look at the color because they said they were done with painting. Steve and I both have allergies to paint, so we were not here for the whole process. We start looking at the paint, and there are two different colors. How is it possible to have two colors? We started asking the painters, but of course, most of them don't speak English. We had to talk to the head painter. Because he did not get all the paint, at the same time, the colors were different. When the store mixed the paint the second time, it was a lighter color. So, they are discussing whose fault it was. If you are a professional painter, you should be able to look at the space and know the amount of paint. We asked them to put two coats of paint on all the walls. It was probably hard to calculate how much would be needed because they usually only paint with one coat.

The painters will come back when they have time and re-paint downstairs. All the rooms upstairs and the bathrooms have all been painted and are the right color. Downstairs on the main level, we had one wall the darker beige and one the lighter beige. You could clearly see they were not the same. The living room, kitchen, dining room, office and hallway with high ceilings will all need to be re-painted with two coats. The painters are not happy and tried to convince us that they were not that much difference in the paint. The paint was not done right so Steve, and I insisted that the bottom floor be repainted.

In the meantime, the carpet has been scheduled to be installed. The floors are starting to get installed and all with no light. We are all a little nervous about the carpets and flooring going in with no light and still painting to be done on the main level. The painters did not have time to come before the hardwoods are installed. So, they will be painting the walls after installation of the hardwood floors.

The inspection for the electric is finally done. Wow so exciting!! I have had to go pick out all new fixtures for the house. A lot of them had smoke damage. We are thankful that the fixture in our dining room was fine. We were a little upset because we have an eat-in area off of our kitchen and the workers lost the pieces to the light. They also broke our Pedestal sink. We have a sink but not a bottom to put the sink on. Steve and I spent lots of time in the store looking for fixtures, ceiling fans, and a new sink. It is exciting to be getting new things but also a lot of pressure. What if I pick something that I don't like and they install it? In the stores, it was so hard to find fixtures as nice as we once had. We looked in stores and online. We could not find a pedestal sink as nice as the one we had before so we decide to get a sink with cabinets for storage. I wanted a place that we could store toilet paper and my rags for cleaning. It was hard to pick out a sink because of the space we have. The bathroom downstairs is a half bath, so it is not very big. We needed the smallest cabinet sink that they made. We finally found a sink cabinet, the size we needed, cherry, and with two drawers. We also had to get ceiling fans on this day. I wanted ceiling fans that had the rod iron look and had intricate details. They were so hard to find, but we finally found three that were all different and the ceiling fans were on sale. We went to the store with a budget from the Contractor. Next, we had to have the Contractor to give us his credit card information so we could get everything we needed. We brought it home and put everything in the closet; so it would all be together.

3-22-17 Finally!!! We have LIGHT!!!! So, exciting!! The inspection finally got approved!! They fixed the wire going to the house. Once we got the inspection approval and the fixtures, we could turn on the lights. We could see again in our house. Because we have electricity that means we have air conditioning. We don't really need it in March, but if we did, we could turn it on. I think we were all in tears with excitement at this point. We are starting to make progress!! We have carpet in the media room and the bedrooms. We have hardwoods in the kitchen, living room, dining room and my office on the main level and now we have light!! We have water!! We can go to the bathroom at our house. Through this process, we could never use our bathroom. We had a portable toilet unit out on our front lawn. My neighbor Pam was always kind enough to let me use the restroom at her house. She would always let me come over even when she wasn't home.

Having Light reminds me that Jesus is the light of the world. Without him, there is darkness, worry, and anxiety. We can shine our light everywhere we go. Matthew 5:16 NIV "Let your light shine before men, that they may see your good works and glorify your Father which is in heaven." We have two choices when we meet people, to be a light or to bring darkness. Our family has smiled and thanked God through every step of the way. We smile when we are out and about in our normal lives. Thinking of others better than ourselves has been our focus during this season and I hope and pray forever. Thanking God for what he saved us from and praising him every day. We are so thankful for God; trusting us with this story and we want to share it with everyone we meet.

We all had peace knowing that God is in control. Our house is a thing that can be replaced. Praying as we deal with the obstacles in life that we are a light into the world for all to see. Is Jesus the light in your life? If not; can you ask Him into your life today? Pray for forgiveness of your sins. Tell Him that you believe in Him and ask Him to be the light of your life.

John 3:16
For God so loved the world, that he gave his only begotten Son, that whosoever believeth in him should not perish, but have everlasting life.

John 8:12 NIV
I am the light of the world. Whoever follows me will never walk in darkness, but will have the light of life.

Journal Entry:
It is my prayer today that others will see the light of God in me.

If you have prayed this prayer and have asked Jesus to be the LIGHT of your life, please seek out a Pastor or a friend that knows him. Begin reading your Bible each day. Psalm is a great place to start. Psalm brings so much hope and so many promises. Hope and pray today that this is a new beginning just as we are getting with our house. A fresh new start.

Our house has been dark, and you could not see without a flashlight. They installed an electrical pole, but until then we had to use flashlights. God is the light of our world. As we see others, we should shine our light into other's lives. Using a flashlight, you can only see what is in front of you. You can't see the surrounding areas. God wants us to follow His light and trust him when we can't see the outcome. We see what is in front of us. When we can see the outcome, we can't trust Him with the unknown. John 12:36 NIV "While you have the light, believe in the light that you may become sons of the light. When we follow His light and trust Him, we are becoming more like Jesus. We can shine God's light of truth into this dark world we live in. Hope and pray today that you will shine your light for all to see.

Our house is starting to look like a home again. There has been so much joy in the process of building a home. You appreciate the fine details that go into building a sturdy, lasting home. We are appreciating having a floor again, being able to use our toilet, carpets, foundation, and having light. Just as building our home has been a process, so is being a Christian. It takes time to get to know God and to live for him. It takes time for him to mold us into the people that He wants us to be. It is a process that cannot be rushed. Sometimes the trials that we go through in life are a part of the process. He is teaching us to rely on Him and to fully trust Him with the intricate details of our lives. Going through trials in life helps you to realize His wonderful power and protection over our lives. God helps you to have peace in trials that no one else can. Praying today, that you will have the peace that comes from having a relationship with God. Praying for peace in the trials you and I are facing. Praying that each step of the way you will fully trust and have faith in God.

John 14:27 (NIV) Peace I leave with you; my peace I give you. I do not give to you as the world gives. Do not let your hearts be troubled and do not be afraid.

CHAPTER TEN
God's Goal

"Not that I have already obtained all this, or have already arrived at my goal, but I press on to take hold of that for which Christ Jesus took hold of me. Brothers and sisters, I do not consider myself yet to have taken hold of it. But one thing I do: Forgetting what is behind and straining toward what is ahead, I press on toward the goal to win the prize for which God has called me heavenward in Christ Jesus."
Philippians 3:12-14 (NIV)

We are getting so excited because our house is starting to come together. We have lights, ceiling fans, floors, and carpets. The cabinets have been installed again with the floors fixed. We still have a fire smell in the stairway to the basement, but the Contractor sprayed something to get rid of the smell. Unfortunately, it only masked it, so we will deal with the smell later. We still have a dumpster in our driveway. We are hoping that the Contractor will leave it there for boxes and items when we move home. We got rid of the green portable potty because we are able to go to the bathroom in our house now! It's the little things like going to the bathroom and turning on lights that we took for granted. Now we appreciate them and are so excited for the blessings God is giving us.

Our goal at this point is to meet the deadline the Contractor gave us. First, the goal was six months after which was Feb 12th. Then it got extended to March 12th, and now because of the water damage in the kitchen, it will take another month and a half. We were all a little disappointed because we were all looking forward to being home. But God gives us His peace knowing that everything happens in his timing, not ours.

> Unless the Lord builds the house,
> the builders labor in vain.
> Unless the Lord watches over the city,
> the guards stand watch in vain.
> Psalm 127:1 (NIV)

The apartment has been nice to live in, and we are all so grateful. It is so convenient to the mall and our Church that we were going to. God has allowed us to take a break from Church. Ashley has volunteered in Ministry for the last six years. I have volunteered with Youth Ministry for three years, and Steve has helped with sound. We have been spending time in the word and been in a season of seeking God for answers in life. This is a season of taking everything that was so important to us away. It is a season of fully relying on God for direction and for Him to guide our steps according to his plans.

The world's goal was for us to get into our house and push to get everything done and get back to "normal." I never want to be normal and be so complacent with life that I forget what is most important. God's goal is most important. It is to have a relationship with Him to grow and be a light to everyone I meet. To truly live a life and be more like Jesus. I also believe that God doesn't want us to resume to our normal lives. God brought us through this process to change us, teach us and to mold us into the people He wanted us to be. God's goal was for us to go through this process, these storms, and encourage and strengthen others. We have been very positive and uplifting to all that we meet. Staying positive and knowing that God has got this and He is in control. Praying that I press on toward the Goal that God has for us.

4-4-17 Met with the fireplace guy to install the fireplace. We are all so excited. The process of picking stones out that would go with our new look has been time-consuming. We had brick in our house before but this time we went with stacked stones that have gray and beige. Everything is so beautiful, and we are so excited to have a stacked stone fireplace. Everything is starting to come together!

It is hard being away from Church, but we have been so hurt by people in Churches. In Churches, we have had so many people not really be there for us. When we met with the Pastor, he even said, "People in the Church tend to hurt you the worst." Why is that? The church is supposed to be family. It is supposed to have people in it that you can run to in times of trouble. In my small group, I had someone say that the Insurance will take care of you. Insurance did give us money, but it was to get equipment so that Steve could get back to work. We did not ask for more than we needed. At the beginning of the fire, we had to eat out, because we didn't have anywhere to cook. There was a lot of unexpected expenses. When we moved in the apartment, they gave us most of what we needed, but we had to buy shampoo, toothpaste etc.

Anything in plastic, in our house, had to be thrown away. We had to cover the cost, and we are supposed to get reimbursed when everything is done.

We have not really experienced the joy of having a Church family. When Steve had cancer, we fought hard together alone with God. We lost his parents six months apart we leaned on each other. We have had family and friends to help us along the way but not a Church family. Trials have made us very strong with our relationship with God and in our marriage.

So, one day, I am praying in the car about a new Church. I love praying in the car. It is my place that I can come to God and seek Him. We have not been going to Church for a few months now, so I asked God, "Where do you want us to go to Church? Over on my right-hand side was a sign that read, "Free Chapel." But God 'Free Chapel' is in Gainesville and it is so far away. I looked online and found a Church in Suwanee the Gwinnett campus, which is near the apartment. So, the next Sunday we attended Church there. I honestly did not like it at first. It was so big, and you watched the Pastor on the screen. It was not what I was used to. It was a great message though. They sure knew how to worship and the Preacher that Sunday was a great Preacher!! So, life got in the way of attending Church the next few weeks. Do you ever have a point in your life that you stop making Church and God a priority? I read my Bible every day, but it is not the same as attending Church, I really don't want to get hurt again. I know that God said to attend "Free Chapel," so we attended, out of obedience. Ashley and I walked in, and one of our favorite singers was there that day, Jason Crabb. Both of us are standing at the back of the Church with tears rolling down our face. We knew we were right where we were supposed to be. Ever have that feeling that you know that God orchestrated your steps and He has you exactly where

He wants you. We knew it that day! This is also the day they "happened" to be talking about Free Chapel College. Free Chapel College? Really? Ashley has been looking for a new direction, and she has been praying about it for quite some time. Ashley and I go check out the college the next day. She applies that same day. She got accepted on Tuesday and was working out the financial aid. She had to also get accepted to Southeastern University because that is the name of the school; Free Chapel was a satellite campus for the school. She gets accepted will start school in August.

God had a goal for our life on 7/24/2017 (her Grandma's birthday that passed away 2009) Ashley's life would forever be changed because we listened to God. Ashley quit her job that week and will start college in August. Ashley is going into Ministry, which she felt like she was called into years ago. She is learning how to have a relationship with God, how to pray and to seek him with her storms in life. She is learning to have a relationship with God and not through me. I have taught her all these years about God, but it is great for her to experience Him in a way that she would never have before the fire. We are all grateful for this amazing opportunity and for God to direct her steps according to his plan; not ours.

God's goal is to draw us near to Him and sometimes that will take us through some struggles in life. God's goal can take us in ways we would have never imagined. He has these amazing plans for all our lives we must trust Him through the process. You may not understand His will and His goal for your life. It is important through the storms in life to seek Him and seek his direction. Cry out to God and ask Him for help. God hears our prayers, and He will direct you according to His plan; take time and listen.

Journal Entry:
Jeremiah 29:11 (NIV) For I know the plans I have for you," declares the Lord, "plans to prosper you and not to harm you, plans to give you hope and a future.

Debbie Morgan's favorite verse:

Proverbs 3:5-6 (NIV) To know God's plan, we must trust him with all our heart. Trust in the Lord with all your heart and lean not on your own understanding; in all your ways submit to him, and he will make your paths straight.

Need to pray before the battle comes. In James, it says we will face trials of many kinds. Make sure you are prayed up and are ready to face God's plan for your life. We start taking inventory of our own strength and abilities. We become discouraged when we don't have what we need for life's trials. God is our source for getting through the trials of life. John 15:5 Apart from me you can do nothing. His power is never-ending, and his wisdom is complete. (inspiration from local Pastor)

CHAPTER ELEVEN
Unexpected Blessings

Consider it pure joy, my brothers and sisters, whenever you
face trials of many kinds, because you know that the testing
of your faith produces perseverance.
James 1:2-3 (NIV)

God blessed us with a direction for Ashley. That was a
truly unexpected blessing that we are truly grateful for.
Ashley knew that she had been called into Ministry since
middle school, but she was not sure how it was going to work
out. So extremely grateful for the blessing of Free Chapel.
Another huge blessing is that we know the children's Pastor
at Free Chapel, from volunteering in theater for many years.
He introduced Ashley to some people the first day of school.
Some of the girls attending college were at the plays we
volunteered for several years ago. They knew Steve and loved
him so much for all the help he gave with the plays. Ashley
started talking to them, and they realized they have been at
plays together for many years. Amazing, when God brings
people back in your life, you never expected.

I took Ashley to a doctor for her headaches from the
concussion. The Neurologist thinks that she should take
some medicine to see if it helps with them. We do not have
insurance right now because we cannot afford it. Steve still
does not have a job, so money for us is tight. Because I have
developed a relationship with the Pharmacist. She knew our
story. She knew we had been through the fire and many
storms in life. I don't talk about them as negative only
positive. I talk to people about how God saved us from the

fire about how good He is. Thanking God in every situation. She found a coupon and gave us half off the medication. So thankful for God's unexpected blessings.

The smoke smell finally got fixed after I called the Insurance company and the contractor out to the house on the same day. I told them the smell starts at the light fixture and goes down to the end of the stairs. Part of the wall was taken out but not the bottom half. The ceiling at the bottom of the stairs was not in the demolition process either. The Contractor and Insurance guy said they would need to take out the wall and the ceiling. When the workers did; that's when they saw black on the drywall. Black from the smoke. That is where the smell was coming from. They removed the drywall and began putting up a new one. Putting new drywall up is very messy work.

I had just cleaned the entire house, and I come home from work, and there is drywall dust everywhere!! I begin to get very frustrated. The Contractor wanted to send someone out to clean our house, but I wanted the house cleaned with a microfiber cloth that removes all the dirt; and no chemicals. I decided to clean it myself because other companies would use chemicals. It is a blessing now because I know it will be clean. It will be a lot of work, but it will be worth it.

One day in the grocery store, I see a neighbor that I have not seen all summer. She asked why haven't you been at the pool? I told her we were not able to pay our homeowners dues yet. For the first time, we set up payment plans for them. Because of the way, the payments were set up, we would not be able to use the pool this year. So, I go about grocery shopping, but I wanted to find her again. I didn't know why it was so important, but I began looking for her. I found her, and she gave me a gift card for the grocery store. She gave a heartfelt gift. I loved her willingness to help us when we needed it. We eventually paid off our dues before the end of the season and were able to go to the pool a couple of times.

Steve and I just celebrated 28 years of marriage. We dated for three years prior to that. Steve is my high school sweetheart. We have been through so many trials before the fire. The enemy had a plan for our marriage and our relationship. The storms we have faced during this season would be enough to break up any marriage. Our relationship with each other is still strong, and Steve is still my best friend. I am forever grateful to God for giving me a partner that will work through the challenges and not give up. We worked so well together through the storms in life. We try our hardest to find something positive. In every situation, there is something positive. Sometimes, it is hard to find but looking on the bright side of things, it's always a blessing. So, when we started having so many problems with the Contractors, we kind of played the 'good cop-bad cop.' If Steve was talking to him (he was the good cop) projects were going ok. If I called and the projects were not going well, (I was the bad cop). Steve did not like handling telling the Contractor there was a problem, so I would talk to him each time. I was not rude to the Contractor but was good at bringing problems to his attention in a positive way.

Our neighbor, Stephanie, noticed how we were handling all the trials we were facing. She had a paper to write on a married couple for school. For instance, the day of the fire, we spent the night at her house. When she came home that night, I said, "Well we have been talking about a spend the night party, so here we are." Steve and I try to make every situation look positive and uplifting. Stephanie chose us to write her paper about our marriage. She interviewed us and wanted to talk about our lives before the fire. What makes our relationship work? The only answer we had was God. When you start your relationship with God; everything else will fall into place. We were so honored to be chosen. It was also a time to tell her about our relationship. We have known her for several years, but there were parts of our story she did not know. It was such a blessing to be able to share our story for such an important paper.

A year and some months later, I get a phone call from a legal representative regarding the litigation. The Insurance company filed a lawsuit against the company that made the gas pipe. The pipe was made way too thin, and the pipe has caused several house fires. The Insurance company won the claim without going to court. This means we don't have to go to court and testify. This also means that we will not be penalized with a claim from the insurance and our premium should not go up. God is so good! So, glad for his favor for our family!

Our vent in our guest bathroom downstairs was crooked. We called the contractor to fix it. That day, an installer, put a hole in the wall in the bathroom. Painters get to come again and paint the bathroom for the third time. The vent is still crooked. They never seemed to manage to get it straight, and after a while, we gave up. The unexpected blessing is that when I use the restroom, I am reminded that all we have been through. I am so glad it is not straight because when people visit our house and ask, I can tell them what God brought us through. It is a reminder of the struggles we faced and how God took us through the storms of life.

Steve has still not found a job and no prospects. He is a very talented man, but no one has called him and no interviews. Steve made a 6-figure income for many years. How are we making it? The story in the Bible with five loaves and two fish comes to mind. Jesus multiplied the food to feed 5,000. Everyone was fed and not hungry. I have been tithing 20 percent of my income from being a Nanny. I have two jobs as a Nanny now, which is good income. When Steve's parents passed away, it was very important to them that we were left with money after they were gone. They pinched pennies and worked so hard to make that happen. We got a distribution check before Steve got laid off. Because they left us money, we could pay off our house in 2010.

During the process of restoring the house; we owned it. So, that is why we really wanted to make sure we got everything fixed correctly. We also have a building that we own in Florida that we get rent checks from each month. God impressed on his parents to save money, and because they did, it is helping us financially through the storms. It still takes money to take care of our home and other expenses, but we are so thankful for the unexpected blessings Steve's parents left for us. I am working two Nanny jobs now. We are very fortunate that both pay well. We still have car insurance for two cars and all the normal bills. God is providing each month, and I am still able to tithe at Church each week. God has been so faithful to us financially. After a long wait, we are also finally getting the check for the contents that were in the house. It is about 1/3 of the total cost to replace what we lost, but we are so grateful. After five months of being home, we can finally buy a couch for downstairs and some of the items that got damaged in the fire. We are all excited because we have not really had appliances. We can bake! One of our favorite blessings is having a rice cooker. Dinner is so easy. You can cook most things in it and leave it for hours. So grateful for the blessings in our home and how God provided for us during this season.

Ashley attended an event with her Dad this year. I planned on going but Aunt Marlene passed away, and I needed to help plan the funeral. It was September 1st, and Steve let someone else drive his mouse droid. He ran right into Ashley's foot, and it was swollen; black and blue. She texted me a picture, and I could not believe how bad it looked. We went to a conference, a few weeks later, and a lady stopped Ashley and asked to put 'Acts 19:11' in her boot and said, 'to walk it out like you have been healed.' God told her at the beginning of the conference that she would receive a miracle. We went to lunch that day, and I told her to take off her boot. Wow, there was such a visible difference!! Her foot looked so much better!! The night before we had danced on it at the Church dance party. It looked like it was gangrene; it looked so bad. I felt like a horrible Mom because I hadn't taken her to the Doctor. She borrowed a boot from a friend for a broken foot. She began telling everyone that she was getting a miracle. She told the Pastor that her foot had been healed. She believed that God was giving her a miracle and He did. Ashley's foot was so much better!! When she took a shower that night, there was no sign of any bruising.

God completely healed her foot!! It says in James, "to bring the Elders of the church and the prayer of faith will heal you." This is exactly what happened! God healed her as no man could do only Him through faith. We have an amazing God and amazing story to share with others! Thankful for the unexpected blessings in life.

Psalm 118:1 O' give thanks unto the Lord; for he is good because his mercy endureth forever.
Psalm 115:15 May you be blessed by the LORD, the Maker of heaven and earth.

We have so many unexpected blessings with our new house. New carpets, new floors, new everything, mostly! We got new comforters for Ashley and our room. New couches for the living room and basement. Our whole house reminds us of the change that happened that day. A fresh new start as Jesus gives us all, when we mess up we can always come to him and repent. God is so loving, and we are so grateful. We now realize that stuff does not matter and now know the importance of having a relationship with God. Things that were important to us before does not matter now. Our relationship with God and each other is the most important thing. We are all so grateful for our new things and new start in life. We are all so grateful for life's unexpected blessings. We do not deserve all that God has brought us through. We are all so undeserving. But thankful for this process and recognizing God's Unexpected Blessings.

Journal Entry:
1 Peter 1:6-7 (NIV) In all this you greatly rejoice, though now for a little while you may have had to suffer grief in all kinds of trials. These have come so that the proven genuineness of your faith—of greater worth than gold, which perishes even though refined by fire—may result in praise, glory, and honor when Jesus Christ is revealed.

Being in need has a way of being an unexpected blessing. When you are in need, you are spiritually seeking God. Looking for answers, only He can provide. People look to things to be their security. When you face trials that we have faced, you find out that your security is in God. We have fully relied on God to be our source of income, and we look to Him to meet our needs. We are now seeking God for his direction and guidance.

He is more reliable than any 401k or any employer. "The Lord is inviting you to trust him and live in both the adventure and security of a life of faith." (Local Pastor).

Trouble comes when we seek to make our own decisions rather than following the leading of God's spirit.

Lord thank you for the generosity and the unexpected blessings. Thank you for providing ALL our needs in such unexpected ways.

Phil 4:9 NIV, My God, will supply all of your needs according to his riches and glory in Christ Jesus.

God is making us all into precious servants who can bring sunshine to the lives of many. We must choose whether we will bring light or darkness to someone. Which will you do; bring someone up when you talk to them or tear them down? You have been chosen to be a blessing to others. The friends in our story brought so much love and comfort to us. It is my prayer that others will realize the impact a simple phone call, a text, a gift card or a prayer can greatly impact someone's life.

Hope and pray that as God blesses you with HIS unexpected blessings. They are all around you. Take time to look and observe. God showed us several throughout our journey. Take time to see the rainbows in life that God gives us all.

CHAPTER TWELVE
God's Discipline

Because the Lord disciplines the one he loves,
and he chastens everyone he accepts as his son. Endure
hardship as discipline; God is treating you as his children.
For what children are not disciplined by their father? If you
are not disciplined—and everyone undergoes discipline—
then you are not legitimate, not true sons and
daughters at all.
Hebrews 12:6-8 (NIV)

Journal entry on 3-19-17
God disciplines the ones he loves to teach, grow stronger in
faith and to renew the relationship. He disciplines us because
he loves us. Discipline sometimes can be painful but so
rewarding. In time, it will produce righteousness and peace. I
had several Christian people ask me what have we done to
make God mad? When you are going through trial after trial,
it does come to mind. But I found comfort in the story of Job.
Job in the bible was being tested even though he had no
unconfessed sin. He remained a person of integrity through
intense trials. Job1:1 says that man was perfect and upright
and one that feared God KJV Job went through lots of trials
and had friends that were not there for him.

Job 31:5-6 NIV If I have walked with falsehood or if my foot
has hastened to deceit. Let me be weighed on honest scales
that I may know my integrity.
God took away "things" that mattered to us in life. He took
us to an apartment for eight months to draw closer to him.

He wanted us all to really get to know him. This was God's discipline for us so he could mold us into the people that he wanted us to be.

God took us through this fire. THROUGH the fire and THROUGH the storm. He didn't leave us in it. He could have decided that we had lived our lives to the fullest that day. But our God chose to take us THROUGH it and teach us his will for our lives. The storms in life was a way of disciplining us but also to help us realize who HE is. Ashley and I love God on such a much deeper level. We have realized what he saved us from and we count our blessings for what he has brought us through. A faith that hasn't been tested is a faith that can't be trusted." Says a pastor on the radio. We learned to have faith through the storms in life. God blesses those that are faithful to him. God disciplines us for our good so that he may be glorified. We have told so many people about God and the fire. It is an open door for us to talk and to tell of his protection.

Just as an earthly father disciplines his son or daughter so does our heavenly Father disciplines us. He loves us, so he is trying to teach us his ways not our own. Proverbs 3:12 because the LORD disciplines those he loves, as a father the son he delights in. In the process of discipline, he is creating us to be more like him.

When you are going through a storm or difficulty in life, it is important to examine your life to see if you have any unconfessed sin. Also, see what changes God may want in your life. Learn through the process. Praise Him through

whatever storm you face. Thank Him for forgiving you. Cry out to God through the storms of life. Sometimes we don't know how to pray but just cry out to Him. God is so faithful even when your future is uncertain. Romans 8:26 declares, "The Spirit helps us in our weakness. WE do not know what we out to pray for, but the spirit intercedes for us."
God may sometimes use trials to test our faith.
1 Peter1:7 NIV, "These trials will show that your faith is genuine. It is being tested as fire tests and purifies gold—though your faith is far more precious than mere gold." So, when your faith remains strong through many trials, it will bring you much praise, glory, and honor on the day when Jesus Christ is revealed to the whole world.

2-19-17 Bible Reading
Proverbs 3:11 NIV, "My son do not despise the Lord's discipline and do not resent His rebuke because the Lord disciplines those He loves as a father does the son he delights in."

1 Peter 3:14 ESV, "But even if you should suffer for the sake of righteousness you are blessed."
1 Peter 17 It is better that you suffer for doing what is right than what is wrong.

My Favorite verse for trials
James 1:2-3 NIV, "Consider it pure joy, my brothers, and sisters, whenever you face trials of many kinds because you know that the testing of your faith produces perseverance. Let perseverance finish its work so that you may be mature and complete, not lacking anything."

This season reminds me of the prodigal son. He wanted all of his inheritance. He spent it all and was eating from troughs. He had to learn the lessons that God had for him. He finally gave his life to his heavenly Father, and his earthly Father welcomed him home with open arms. He was lost in his ways, but now he is found.

The prodigal son had to learn through his trials and learn from his mistakes. We learned that God disciplines the one He loves, and the testing of our faith produces perseverance. These trials are helping us to be mature Christians and not baby Christians. Trials have deepened our relationship with God, and we realize because of His discipline He loves us. Proverbs 10:17 (NIV) Whoever heeds discipline shows the way to life, but whoever ignores correction leads others astray.

David's life was full of trials, temptation, forgiveness, and sin. God spared him of his life choices. God protected him every step of the way. David did not realize at the time that God was molding him into the person He wanted him to be. David was a Shepard, a psalmist, ruler and a leader. Sometimes it's through the trials that God changes our perspective in our lives.

Some of us are in similar situations of trials and temptation. The question is, "Do we believe God is in control? If He's not, then who is?" In other words, if life events are random and without purpose, then to whom do we turn in trials?" (local Pastor)

In 1st Chronicles 29:12, David says that God rules over everything and His hand strengthens everyone.

Have faith in the Lord's ability to strengthen you. Though you may not always understand His reasons, you can surely trust His promises and will for your life.

Journal Entry:

We have had so many trials through this fire. Workers have been making mistakes. I am asking myself today, "Am I being obedient to God?" Psalm 84:11 NIV, "No good thing will He withhold for those that walk uprightly." Am I walking uprightly? Am I walking and living a life according to his will? According to the world, bad things keep happening to us. Yet, I think, God is giving us many opportunities to show our faithfulness to Him.

Job 31:5-6 NIV, "If I have walked with falsehood or if my foot has hurried to deceit let me be weighed on honest scales that I may know that I am blameless."

Lord disciplines for our good, so He may be glorified.

The motive to discipline is Love.

Psalm 37:18-19, "Hardships, trials, disaster, and famine will come and go. But God's faithfulness and promise to keep us, are eternal." Therefore, we can rest in the security of knowledge that we can trust God with everything.

Spiritual Growth: Seeing life differently. Having His PEACE in our lives through our storms.

CHAPTER THIRTEEN
What Do You Believe?

The steps of a good man are ordered by the LORD:
and He delighteth in his way.
Psalm 37:23 (KJV)

Do you believe God sent the lightning that day? It says in the Bible that God created the world. Do you know how God controls the clouds and makes his lightning flash? (Job 37:15). In Luke, it says "even the winds and the waves obey him." Why did God send us the lightning strike that day? Why our family? I am honored to have had this trial. Apparently, He thought our family would be strong enough to endure it. Many families would have struggled with the many storms we faced. The only way we got THROUGH them was with God. He walked us every step of the way. This verse helped encourage me in 1st Corinthians 10:13, "No temptation has overtaken you except what is common to mankind. And God is faithful; He will not let you be tempted beyond what you can bear. But when you are tempted He will also provide a way out so that you can endure it."

We were all not supposed to be home that night. We had practice for Sunday Church, but we all decided to stay home. We are never usually in the same room. Do you believe God placed it in our hearts that we did not need to go to Church that evening? I do. We very rarely miss Church and practice. Steve runs the sound and Ashley, and I sing in the choir. God directed our steps that night according to his plans. I feel like He wanted us home, so we could all be together. So that we could face this storm together. It has strengthened our relationship with each other in ways that only God could have done. It strengthened our relationship with each other and did not destroy us, which is what the enemy intended. Do you believe God tries to get our attention? In the Old Testament of the Bible, Bible, people were not acting like God wanted them to. He asked Noah to build a boat for his families and the animals. Noah worked on the boat for a long time. God sent a flood, and the only ones that were safe were Noah and his family. Noah was obedient to God. There are a lot of storms in life, and if you are not living the way God wants you to, He might try to redirect your attention. I know that through these storms He has redirected us to what is important in life. His desire for us as Christians is to learn to depend on him so that in our weakness, He will be strong. (quote from Charles Stanley).

Isiah 40:31, When we wait on the Lord He Promises to renew our strength!

During this season, at the Church we were attending, the Pastor got up and talked about Baptism. He told us that in the Old Testament, the Bible says to baptize the whole family including babies. They referred to Acts 16:31. They replied, "Believe in the Lord Jesus, and you will be saved--you and your household." This scripture says "believe." How can a baby believe? How does a baby know what is happening when he is sprinkled?

At the Church, we are attending they believe in sprinkling babies not many adults. At first, I did not have a hard time with it because it is not the water that saves you. Confessing and believing in the Lord Jesus Christ is what saves you and makes you a believer. As I get into the scripture more, I realize that sprinkling a baby is not Biblical. Romans 10:9-10 NIV, "If you declare with your mouth, "Jesus is Lord," and believe in your heart that God raised him from the dead, you will be saved. 10 For it is with your heart that you believe and are justified, and it is with your mouth that you profess your faith and are saved." These scriptures are talking about confessing and believing which are two things I don't believe babies can do. The Pastor also talked about that John Wesley baptized, an infant, three times many years ago. The baby got pneumonia and died, and that is why they believe in sprinkling instead of dunking in water. This is the point of why we stopped going to Church and started getting into the word and finding out what we believe. I feel like God called us to a time of fully relying on Him and to find out what we believe. We were taken away from so many things that were important to us. Ashley did not have her piano or her music. Steve did not have his workshop, his job or Geekspace any longer. This was a time for us to 'be still and know that He is God.'

Most importantly do you believe that Jesus died on the cross for your sins and mine? John 3:16-17 NIV, "For God so loved the world that he gave his one and only Son, that whoever believes in him shall not perish but have eternal life. 17 For God did not send his Son into the world to condemn the world, but to save the world through him". God died on the cross for your sins and mine. If you believe in him and ask forgiveness of your sins, He can come into your life today.

God sent us many storms this past year, and He will continue to give us storms. God is our Protector, and in whom we can trust. It is important that through this storm and circumstances that we remain faithful. He knows the plans he has for each of us, and we must trust him with the details. He created the heavens and the earth. He creates lightning, floods, and storms. These storms in life may test our faith and to bring us closer to Him, if we trust Him through the process. When God brings you to a trial or situation, He equips you for it. What He brings you to; He will bring you through. We must be willing to stand for Christ, no matter our circumstances.

Deuteronomy 31:8 NIV, "The LORD himself goes before you and will be with you; he will never leave you nor forsake you. Do not be afraid; do not be discouraged."

Journal Entry:
Mark 16:16 (NIV) Whoever believes and is baptized will be saved.
John 3:16 (NIV) For God so loved the world that he gave his one and only Son, that whoever believes in him shall not perish but have eternal life.

Galatians 2:20 (NIV) I have been crucified with Christ, and I no longer live, but Christ lives in me. The life I now live in the body, I live by faith in the Son of God, who loved me and gave himself for me.

Romans 10:9 (NIV) If you declare with your mouth, "Jesus is Lord," and believe in your heart that God raised him from the dead, you will be saved.

God should not be our last resort when we are faced with adversity. We should seek him first, and he will guide us in the way HE wants us to go.

Matthew 6:33 (NIV) Seek first the Kingdom of God and his righteousness and ALL these things shall be added to you. Matthew 6:25 (NIV) Therefore, do not worry about tomorrow for tomorrow will worry about itself. Vs. 34 Each day has enough trouble of its own.

Whose kingdom are you living for? If you worry about food, clothing, health, you are more concerned with OUR kingdom more than God's.

Focus on HIS will, rather than your desires. Refuse to let worry steal the joy of walking with God

We are free to do what GOD calls us to. It is an honor to serve Jesus. Our life is not about us. We are to serve one another just as Christ would do.

CHAPTER FOURTEEN
Moving Back Home

I sought the LORD, and He heard me,
and delivered me from all my fears.
Psalm 34:4 (KJV)

And we know that in all things God works for the good of
those who love him, who have been called according to his
purpose.
Romans 8:28 (NIV)

April 25, 2017, is Moving Day! We are all very excited to
be moving home. We will not have all our belongings, but we
will be home tonight. Today, the Contents company will
come at 10:00 to start moving the items from the apartment.
The Rental company will come to pack up dishes and linens
also; at the same time. The Contents company comes, and it
is the four girls! Ashley and I are so excited to see them! We
start to go over all of the items that need to be moved. We
bought beds instead of having the rental furniture. So, both
of our mattresses need to be moved. There are a lot of people
with the Contents company. They have about seven people,
and then there are also two people packing rental items.
Ashley and I are there also; so this is an enormous amount of
people for the little apartment.

As they begin taking the boxed items, I show them the
elevator. They were so excited to have an elevator because we
were on the 5th floor. The stairs would be hard to climb each
time. The Supervisor told us that they could only take boxed
items. We accumulated quite a bit of stuff in 8 months. We

had computers, tables, clothes, Christmas items that people gave us and some appliances. My husband worked from the apartment; so we had all his equipment there. Even though he got laid off in January, we still had some of the things he worked with. We also bought a teal and coral comforter to add color to the apartment. Along with colorful pillows to match. Of course, we collected a few Star Wars Items too. One of the trips to the elevator included the 3 ft. Darth Vader and a Stormtrooper. We had lots of fun taking selfies of these special moments. We did not realize that all the items had to be packed in a box. The Contents company's personnel were very kind to us. They actually took some stuff that was not boxed and there was still an enormous amount of work for us to do at the apartment.

Next, Steve would meet the Contents company at the storage unit to get everything out of it. The electronics company wanted to clean a lot of the equipment at the beginning of this process. Steve knew it would probably not work, so he had a storage unit for some of our clothes, his equipment, and our wave runner.

So, Ashley and I go to our home and start getting ready for them to deliver the apartment items and storage. While we were at the apartment, our couches were delivered. They are beautiful, very comfy, grey couches. We are both so happy to have a comfortable couch to sit on! We are all so excited because we can charge our phones on the side of the couch, as well. They are powered, and they look so nice with the grey countertops in kitchen.

The Contents company starts pulling up to the house with two vans full. We have three or four guys and six girls. That is a lot of people. Each time a person goes in the house, they have to take off their shoes, because our hard floors have not cured long enough yet. So, some of the girls would just take the boxes in the house, so everyone didn't have to take off their shoes every time. They have lots of boxes. They would ask 'where it goes' and I would say, 'basement' for most boxes. Most of the boxes were from Steve's office. We did not have many clothes at the apartment and lived on the bare minimum for those eight months.

We were all so thrilled that the girls thought to bring our refrigerator. We did not bring our refrigerated items from the apartment because we didn't think we would have a refrigerator. When they go to set up the frig, the bolts were missing. So, we have two people holding the front side of the frig until the parts were found. Everyone is looking everywhere, but no one could find them. This took about an hour trying to find the parts. One of the guys improvised and somehow got the frig together. We were not sure the frig would work because all the other items that were plugged into outlets have not worked. They plug it in and get the water line set up. It works! We are all so happy to have a nice big refrigerator!

It was starting to feel like home when they set up our beds. Except Ashley did not have a bed frame for her bed because she had the rental frame at the apartment. She did not care because she was glad to be home. We did not have TV's that work. We had beds and a couch. We all felt so blessed!!

While the Contents company is bringing boxes, the Housing man calls, to ask me why I am not at the apartment. We got so busy with directing boxes that I forgot I was supposed to meet the Rental company at 3:00. Thankfully, I could give my permission to the staff at the apartment complex, and they let them in. They took all the furniture and household items. While the Contents company is moving boxes, a Decorator came by from the furniture company. It is a free service they offer if you buy their couches. She was helping me to determine what chairs I could use for one of the walls in living room. She suggested two swivel chairs for the area and a small table to sit between the chairs. She also helped me with a color scheme for our new living room. She showed me pillows that would tie the whole look together. I have always wanted a decorator to help coordinate our house. So exciting and it is so hard to believe it is free!!

Finally, everyone left. We have lots of boxes, but we begin to put things away from out of the boxes. On Saturday, we must get everything out of the storage unit and the apartment. The Contents company did not take clothes and anything not boxed up. We would normally, use a sturdy blue wagon when moving stuff from the apartment but it is gone with R2. We also signed up for a fundraiser for foster kids, and a friend took R2 for us (so we could keep our word). So, since the wagon is gone, we have to carry everything by hand from the fifth floor. We have an elevator, but it is a long walk when carrying so much. Thankfully, we got out of the apartment and the storage unit both by Sunday. It was an enormous amount of work to do, but we got it done.

Over the weekend, we are finally home, but we do not have any dishes or silverware. We bought paper plates and plastic silverware to get us by. We have one pot and one frying pan; it was perfect for cooking. I enjoyed the simple life at the apartment and the smaller amount of stuff that we had. So being home with less stuff is kind of nice. With all the boxes and smells it was very hard to sleep. We have a smell from our clothes that were restored. It smells like chemicals. All of the clothes will need to be washed in vinegar to get the smell out. We also have the smell of the basement. Ashley and I won't go down there because the smell is so bad. You open the door to the basement, and you can immediately smell the smoke smell. Because everything had its own distinguished smell, it was quite motivating to get the boxes unpacked, and clothes washed. It is a great comfort being home, but my mind is racing with all that needs to be accomplished. I try praying and reading scripture, and that begins to help.

Monday comes, and the Contents company delivers 300 boxes and all the furniture. For the main level, nothing can go on the floors yet. So, everything goes in the garage instead of individual rooms. They give us time to unpack all these boxes, and then they bring the remaining boxes a week later. We are all so grateful that we had this time to go through boxes in stages. First the apartment boxes. 300 boxes, furniture and then the remaining boxes. As we start unpacking some of the boxes, we could not believe it. The boxes were not full they had lots of paper around them. At first, it was kind of frustrating, but then we realized we could unpack boxes quickly since most of the time the boxes had only a few items in it. Also, the Restoration company restored everything, but they did not know what items went together. So, you might have items from the living room with items from the sewing room. They were pretty good about keeping things together, for the most part, but we did have a lot of stuff!

While we are living back in the house, we have workers that still need to come to finish it. The basement is not complete. We have walls and carpets, but none of the equipment for the movie room has been set up yet. The first night at the house, we have couches, and we have a TV but no sound because it has not been installed. The installers of the electronics came with all of the equipment, and they bring this really large screen. There is no way that screen is going to fit. They begin to measure, and it is too big! So, they have to order another screen for the movie room. Steve does not like some of the equipment that they bring, so they would have to return that as well. He was very specific at the beginning of the project what he wanted, but some of the equipment is hard to get now. For example, Steve had an R2D2 Xbox that is virtually impossible to get now. The company is doing a really good job working with Steve to get equipment back the way it was with a lot of improvements. We have a nice projector, that is now mounted on the back of the wall, so it cannot be seen.

We have had lightning hit the projector two other times, so we wanted to make sure that we got a good one this time. Each day we are not sure what time workers will come. One morning we had workers come at 8:30 to work on the punch list. The guy shows up to the house with his girlfriend. She is obviously not a worker because I saw them kissing on our lawn. She follows him around everywhere he goes, but she is not working. They are supposed to install an attic fan, and he came up to me and told me the Contractor would have to get someone else because he did not know how to install it. They did fix a cement area on the driveway and then left. They were not here long.

The second day of the HVAC guys (electronic guys): They begin hooking up speakers and show me how to use our universal remote. The remote controls the TV, lights and the garage. Pretty neat and very simple! He also showed us that everything is wireless and that the DVD is in the closet now. We are all so extremely excited that we have sound! We can hear the Apple TV. We don't have cable now, but we have an Apple TV with Netflix. We go downstairs to check out the movie room. They have installed most of the equipment.

They have also installed the screen so that we can watch movies. He starts to bring the screen down, and the screen looks great until it gets all the way down. The screen is not exactly straight at the top of the screen. It is a diagonal line. They are not sure what happened, so they call the company and realize that it is a manufacturing error. Again, they will have to order a new screen. Because of the mix-ups with the screens, we will be getting a much nicer screen. The screen company wanted to make sure we were taken care of.

Moving home was a little overwhelming because the amount of stuff we had. We all had a hard time remembering where things went. There were some items we asked where did this come from? This was not in our house? Some of the things we had were now on our discard list. Anything that was ruined in the fire had to be on a discard list and have pictures of each item. Our discard list was quite extensive. In our bathroom, we have plastic shampoo bottles, lotions, and medicines. We had to get rid of all of it. The nice thing about moving home is that the space we used in the apartment is the space we use at home. We have a big bathroom with four drawers and two side cabinets. We only use two drawers and the cabinets. We don't have a bunch of lotions and medicines anymore. We all want to keep it simple and less cluttered.

Our closet area was packed before the fire with not much space for any more clothes. It is a huge walk-in closet. Now we do not have as many clothes, and it is now color coordinated. We gave clothes and things we did not want to the homeless. Living in an apartment showed us what was important. We sold our boat, got rid of skis and all the items for the Lake. God showed us how much we could live without and how to be grateful for all he has given us.

In our kitchen, when unpacking, we decided to set aside dishes and items Ashley could use when she moves out. We had two of almost everything in the kitchen; so, we leave items packed that Ashley could use. We also left the China her Grandma left for her. It is an 8-piece setting of white China, that will go with anything. When we move back, we do not have any of our appliances. Except for the coffee machine. I had to have that in the apartment! We had two pots and a frying pan which was just perfect for what we needed. We needed to purchase a lot for the house, but Steve does not have a job yet. I am working two Nanny jobs, but it is helping to pay our bills. Our Adjustor was supposed to send us a check for the contents. After we moved home, we had to list each item in our house, the location and the age.

This process is very overwhelming, and it takes weeks to list and input into their spreadsheet. We had a list of items and took pictures, but it had to be entered in their program. We should have been inputting this information while at the apartment but we always seemed to have too much going on. It took us about 12 weeks to enter information and to get a check from the Insurance company. When we got the check, it was 1/3 of the cost to replace items. After we purchase items, we have to send receipts to the insurance company, and they will at the point give us replacement value. We only have two years to complete this process, and it has already been a year. Since we do not have money, we live in our house without. We are all so grateful to be home and realize stuff doesn't matter. We are what makes our home; 'people' and our relationship with each other. Building the love and friendships even with adversity is the one thing that makes our house a home.

Our living room and our main level are so nice now all with hardwood floors. The hardwood floors make the room look so much bigger. Our living room has speakers in the ceiling, so none of the wires are showing. We have a white ceiling and white speakers, so it is hard to see the speakers. Our TV is mounted above our fireplace now. The wires are behind the wall. We got new end tables so that we can charge our phones. Steve installed a unit in our couch that we can charge phones and plug in our remote. For quite some time, we had an extension cord across the living room floor for plugging into the couch. Steve installed a plug in the floors that would be underneath the couch so it would not show.

The kitchen, eat-in area, and living room are all open to each other. We have a speaker now in the ceiling that will play music from your phone. It is so nice to listen to music and cook. We have speakers on the back deck now, and you can also hear the music or TV out on the deck. One night, we came home, and it was very late. We heard this loud music. It was blaring so loud. We walk in our house and realize it is coming from our back deck. How did the system turn on? None of us turned it on. It was weird, but Steve found a way to disconnect the system until we could get HVAC guy out. He installed a special system called Control 4 and the lights. The Garage, TV and pretty much everything is controlled by this system. You can also access the system with your phone. Along with this system is a camera at the front door. We can answer the door with our phone. You can talk to the person or let the person in. We can see when packages come. One time we saw a package being thrown on the front porch.

The one thing I prayed for was our pictures. Most of the albums and pictures all look good. We have an enormous number of pictures on the walls and in albums. One picture changed a lot! It was a mountain scene with a bear. Now the trees are blue, water is blue, and the bear is blue. I loved this picture but now our décor has changed, and we can get something new. I have taken a few pictures of our family and put them around the house. One of my family and one of Steve's family. One special picture is the last time we went to a dinner with Melayne. July 16, 2016, right before the fire. Who knew this would be our final picture altogether? We all find great comfort in the picture because we are all so happy together. We have pictures of my brother's five foster children. They have been such a blessing to our lives, and we are so grateful for the joy they bring our family. Photos are important to all of us, and we are grateful for the ones we have. Right now, we are so overwhelmed with the number of pictures. We have been married almost 29 years. That is an enormous amount of pictures! The pictures that I came back for during the fire was Ashley's baby book. All the pictures are fine and with no smell. We are all so blessed that they survived the fire and we have the special memories to look back on.

As we move back home and start to get settled, we all start to be an emotional mess. Why now? We have been through so much, and we are home. Why are we all sad? We realize we never had time to grieve Melayne. After she passed away, we moved into the house and was going through the motions of life. Do you ever have a time of going through motions? We all must take time to grieve. Even Jesus had a time of sadness. John 11:35 NIV, Jesus Wept. We lost a lot of family during the fire, but we never had time to process. We lost my Uncle Gerald, Aunt Clara, Aunt Marlene and lots of friends during the fire. It took quite some time to grieve and to process all that we had been through with these storms in life. This season of grief is a time of focusing on God and crying out to him. He is the only one that can help us with the grief we are all dealing with.

We are all so grateful to be home! Even through all the trial and storms we faced, we are all still best of friends. This has helped us all work together instead of working against each other. My parents and friends have helped so much through these trials. I will be forever grateful. We learned through the storms in life that each storm is different, but you must approach them all the same way. Trusting in God and having faith that "He works all things together for your good." Romans 8:28 NIV, God is in control, and he has your best interest at heart. God tested our faith through these trials and brought us through each one.

Journal Entry:
Storms in life are going to come and go. It is important to keep your faith through these storms in life. Keep your eyes on God and not your circumstances. Read the Psalms when you are weary and discouraged. We are to seek and to set our desires on Spiritual matters. To seek what God wants for each of our lives.

3-20-17
Ephesians 6:10-11 (KJV) Be strong in the Lord and in the power of his might. Put on the whole armor of God that you may be able to stand against the devil's schemes.

Our Faith in Jesus makes us safe in the Lord's care. Only strength of God can win the war against Satan.

Put on the Full Armor:
Belt of Truth, Breastplate of Righteousness, Shoes of Peace, Shield of Faith, Helmet of Salvation, Sword of the Spirit (Bible).

Thank you for your strength God through the storms of life. Thank you for the fire and the trial you have given us. Thank you for your discipline and your love.
God finishes what He starts!

Thank you for a new start and new beginnings. Thank you for your blessings each day. Pray that as we begin our new start that we do not go back to the former ways. Thank you for entrusting us with this powerful story. Thank you for not giving up on us and loving us even with our imperfections.

Thank you for starting a good work in all of us. Thank you for changing our lives forever!! Pray that we each will seek you earnestly each day. Pray for Steve as he guides and leads our family. Pray that you guide our steps today and every day according to your will. Pray that we all keep our eyes on you. Pray that we will always seek you with our heart and soul. Help us all not to get distracted by our circumstance. God thank you for being bigger than our circumstances!

Psalm 34:18-19 (NIV) The Lord is near to those who have a broken heart and saves those who are crushed in spirit. The righteous person may have troubles, but the Lord delivers him from the ALL!!

Hebrew11:1 (KJV) Now faith is the substance of things hoped for, the evidence of things not seen: vs. 6 But without faith, it is impossible to please him: for he that cometh to God must believe that he is, and that he is a rewarder of them that diligently seek him.

CHAPTER FIFTEEN
Forever Changed

Praise the LORD, my soul;
all my inmost being, praise his holy name.
Praise the LORD, my soul,
and forget not all his benefits—
who forgives all your sins
and heals all your diseases,
who redeems your life from the pit
and crowns you with love and compassion,
who satisfies your desires with good things
so that your youth is renewed like the eagle's.
Psalm 103:1-5 (NIV)

Therefore, if any man be in Christ, he is a new creature: old things are passed away; behold, all things are become new.
2 Corinthians 5:17 (KJV)

The enemy had a plan for our lives on 8/18/2016, but GOD had a different plan. He planned to change our lives in a way that could never be imagined. He chooses to reveal himself to us through the fire and through the storms in life. Storms in life will still come. I have learned to keep my focus on Jesus and not my circumstances. My God is bigger than my circumstances and what is going on around me!! I knew God before but not this God. The God that turns the sorrow and the trials into learning more about him. This God helped me in ways that no one could have ever done.

I learned so much through the fire. One is to not take life for granted. None of us know when our last breath could be.

Each day we should live for him and tell others about him. The day of the fire according to the world should have been our last day here on earth. Gas fumes are everywhere in the basement. The world says that it should have blown up. But God protected us in a way that only he could have. He saved us from the fire and allowed us to see his light shining through the fire. We did not know that our time with Melayne would be so short. We must hold onto the precious memories we have with our family and friends. It is important to let them know you love them and to make time for them. Cherish the time you have with family and friends. Don't take life for granted. Thank and praise God for each day he gives you and your family.

Second, I learned to keep my eyes and focus on God. God is so much bigger than our circumstances. We all have a choice each day to live for God or for the enemy. You can choose to face a trial with God's word. We could have been angry and said, "why me?" Instead, we chose to live a life for God and to be a witness to him through the storm. God works all things for our good, and I know he will take care of us with every storm that comes our way. He wanted to be our protector our provider. He revealed himself to us. He gave us this amazing story to share for the rest of our lives. What if Paul and David in the Bible had not shared their story? We would have some important stories missing. God asked me to write this story. I couldn't have written it if I hadn't gone through it. God wanted me to share this story to encourage and to lift others through the storms in life.

Be thankful for everything! We all have so much stuff. It is amazing what we can live without. Be thankful God has blessed you with lights, water, couches, etc. Be thankful for the little things in life that you assume you will have daily. We were all so excited to see Light in our house. Jesus is the light of our life, and we can share his light with people we meet. There is no darkness with him. We may go through hard times, but God is molding us into the people that he wants us to be.

We also learned that it helps to have good insurance. We are also grateful for our insurance and our insurance company. The house cost about $166,000 to repair. We are so thankful for each company that helped us with the contents of our home. To pack up the clothes and bring them back was about $13,000.00. When the clothes came back, they had a chemical smell. None of us could stand the smell. Each clothing item had to be rewashed in vinegar and detergent. That was a lot of work washing all the clothes, linens and comforters. We gave our comforter and matching curtains away to a needy family because we couldn't get the chemical smell out. We also gave them our headboard and footboard. We currently do not have one but feel so blessed to be home. Our room is so quiet and dark compared to the apartment. The apartment faced a parking lot, so you heard every time someone came home. Our bedroom at the apartment had a street light outside of it, so it was never dark. Our house is nice and quiet, and we are all so happy to be home.

The electronics company that picked up the equipment cost about $16,000. We got back about 10,000 of the money because we chose not to have it cleaned or tested since it did not work. We replaced the TV, Apple TV's and lots of electronic equipment. Steve set up an area in the garage and tested the equipment himself. He retrieved the pictures from the computers. He spent hours trying to see what equipment worked. Most of the computers, TV's, and equipment were ruined.

The Contents company cost an enormous amount of money. For the company to come and pack up our items, clean them and bring them back home was about $94,000. The insurance company paid a storage fee for each item for eight months. Again, we learned during this process the importance of having good insurance. We learned that it is also cheaper to repair than to rebuild. We learned that these companies charge an enormous amount of money but that they are good at restoration. At the beginning of this process, we were told we would get a depreciation check for the house, but the $40,000, this money went to the construction company. Still, don't understand why that went to them and not us but we had to trust God with the process. Because we were in the apartment an extra month beyond our contract, we had to pay for the last month of rent for the apartment. This was our deductible for the insurance company. Each check for the construction and restoration came to us to pay the company. Lots of checks went to each company. We did not get our contents check until months after we moved in the house. So, because Steve did not have a job, there were things we did without. The insurance company did give us money initially to get Steve back to work, but all the money went toward his equipment.

For us to get our contents check, we had to list each item that was in our house. The contents company took pictures at the time of the fire, but it was our responsibility to enter each item in the computer. This took quite some time. We did not start the process until we moved back home and could see what items we got back. We had to list each item, tell its age, where we bought it, the year we bought it and the condition of each item in our house. We had an enormous amount of stuff, so this took some time to sort out this process. We finally after six months of living at home could replace our couches downstairs and some of the items we lost. As we approach the Christmas season, we will need to buy all new items. We only have two years to complete the process of getting our stuff replaced for insurance purposes.

It has already been a year since the fire happened. We got our contents check, and it is 1/3 of the amount it will take to replace the items. At this point, we must buy the item, and if it exceeds the amount the insurance company gave us, then we have to turn in receipts. Then we will hopefully and prayerfully we will get another distribution check for the additional money we have spent. We have learned through this process to document each item that you have in your house and keep receipts! Take pictures or shoot video. We had a lot of expensive items, and it was hard to convince the insurance company it's value. For instance, the Lego pirate ship was about a $100 when we bought it, and it cost a $1,000.00 to replace it today. The Legos could not be cleaned, so we don't have $1000.00 to replace it so this is one item that we will not get to replace. This is one item, and there are thousands of items in our house. We know stuff does not matter but, it can be quite overwhelming at times the significant amount of stuff and memories we lost. We lost a great deal of special memories but gained so much more. We have a deeper relationship with God and know His true power. This is something priceless that we will cherish for eternity.

I pray that as you look at the foundation of your home that you keep your foundation in Christ. Having a good relationship with Christ creates a good foundation in your home. If you center your home around God, then everything else will be directed according to God's plans for your life. Focusing on the circumstances is fear, not faith. Faith is whatever the circumstance, not matter how bad things look that our God is faithful. Hebrews 11:16 Faith is the substance of things hoped for the evidence of things not seen. Vs. 6 But without faith, it is impossible to please him: for he that cometh to God must believe that he is and that he is a rewarder of them that diligently seek him. When you see your foundation of your home, you have faith that it is secure and will hold the rest of your house. Know that if our foundation is in Christ, he will reward those that diligently seek him.

Our home looked good from the outside, and it did not appear that we had a fire. In the basement, it was covered in soot. Most of our things got damaged in the basement. We have all learned that things do not matter. Things can be replaced. We learned that our relationship with God, each other, and our friends are the most important. God can help us all with the mess in our lives. He can restore you and help you to be joyful during the most difficult times in your life. Joy is a sign of a healthy Christian fully relying on God. God is the only one that can help you overcome difficulties and trials.

We had many storms through the fire. One thing we did learn is to think of others better than ourselves. We continued to do charity throughout this whole process. Almost every weekend we were at a troop or visiting the hospitals. This was our way of giving back to others. Taking the focus off us and focusing on someone else. It turns out the problems we had were fixable. There are children with cancer-fighting every day to live. Our problems seemed so small. We got to raise money for a group of kids to go to Disney. It was so much fun getting to be a part of such wonderful charities. Focusing and helping others turns your attention to their needs. This made us all feel so much better. Learning to see obstacles as opportunities. God allowed us to share His story with so many because of the challenges we faced. We could tell others about His protection and His love. It was an opportunity for us to share our story and show others the amazing amount of faith and positive attitude we had through these storms. It was a story of faith, hope, and love. God wanted us to face these challenges but have faith through them. Faith that He would see us through them every step of the way. God was at work in our lives in ways we could have never imagined. Praying as we all face the storms in life that we use these storms as opportunities to tell others about Jesus and to tell others of the JOY we have.

"God is more reliable than work or any employer. The Lord is inviting you to trust him and live in both the adventure and security of life of faith." Charles Stanley. Being in need can have its benefits. People look to things as security. But when you go through the storms in life, security is in Him. He is our refuge and our strength, and in Him we trust.

We are all extremely grateful for our new start in life. We lost a lot of sentimental stuff but gained so much more. Our house and the stuff in it is all brand new. We have a new life that God has given us. Our relationship with God is so much stronger now. We know what it means to fully rely on God. Steve is home everyday building and creating projects. Ashley is attending college, and she loves it! It is a perfect fit for her. She is so excited about this ministry opportunity. It is cool how God gave her instant friends. I have two Nanny jobs now, and I love pouring love into both of them. R2 has a new drive system, and he can now drive in the grass. We are all having so much fun with R2 now. We had many storms in our lives, but God knew how this story would end. He knew the plans he had for all of us. Storms in life will come and go. It is important to keep your faith through them all. Trust in God, and he will see you Through the Storms in life.

JOURNALING THROUGH THE STORM
Inspiring scriptures during our journey

Whatever circumstance you are in, God is with you and will carry you through it.

Challenges requires faith and trust that no matter the circumstances that come your way you remain faithful to God

Psalm 138:7-8 (NKJV)
Though I walk in the midst of trouble, you will revive me;
You will stretch out Your hand
Against the wrath of my enemies,
And Your right hand will save me.
The LORD will perfect *that which* concerns me;
Your mercy, O LORD, *endures* forever;
Do not forsake the works of Your hands.

Psalm 28:7 (NIV) The LORD is my strength and my shield;
my heart trusts in him, and he helps me.
My heart leaps for joy, and with my song I praise him.

Psalm 136:1 (NIV) Give thanks to the LORD, for he is good.
His love endures forever.

Psalm 27:14 (NIV) Wait for the LORD; be strong and take heart and wait for the LORD.
Psalm 91 (KJV) No evil shall befall you. Nor shall any plaque come near your dwelling for he shall give his angels charge over you to keep you in all of your ways.

Psalm 55:16 (NIV) I will call upon God and the Lord shall save me. Evening, morning and at noon I will pray and cry aloud and he hears my voice.

Psalm 142 (KJV)
I cried unto the LORD with my voice; with my voice unto the LORD did I make my supplication.
2 I poured out my complaint before him; I shewed before him my trouble.
3 When my spirit was overwhelmed within me, then thou knewest my path. In the way, wherein I walked have they privily laid a snare for me.
4 I looked on my right hand, and beheld, but there was no man that would know me: refuge failed me; no man cared for my soul.
5 I cried unto thee, O LORD: I said, Thou art my refuge and my portion in the land of the living.
6 Attend unto my cry; for I am brought very low: deliver me from my persecutors; for they are stronger than I.
7 Bring my soul out of prison, that I may praise thy name: the righteous shall compass me about; for thou shalt deal bountifully with me.

Psalm 145:18- 19 (NIV)
18 The LORD is near to all who call on him,
 to all who call on him in truth.
19 He fulfills the desires of those who fear him;
 he hears their cry and saves them.

Psalm 84:11 (KJV)
For the LORD God is a sun and shield: the LORD will give grace and glory: no good thing will he withhold from them that walk uprightly

Psalm 9:9-10 (NIV)
The LORD is a refuge for the oppressed,
 a stronghold in times of trouble.
Those who know your name trust in you,
 for you, LORD, have never forsaken those who seek you.

Psalm 5:11-12 (NIV)
But let all who take refuge in you be glad;
let them ever sing for joy.
Spread your protection over them,
that those who love your name may rejoice in you.
 Surely, LORD, you bless the righteous;
 you surround them with your favor as with a shield.

Psalm 18:2-3 (NIV)
The LORD is my rock, my fortress and my deliverer;
my God is my rock, in whom I take refuge,
my shield and the horn of my salvation, my stronghold.
I called to the LORD, who is worthy of praise,
and I have been saved from my enemies.

Philippians 1:6 (NIV)
being confident of this, that he who began a good work in you will carry it on to completion until the day of Christ Jesus.

www.ingramcontent.com/pod-product-compliance
Lightning Source LLC
La Vergne TN
LVHW021342080426
835508LV00020B/2077